WORLD OF VOCABULARY

PURPLE

Sidney J. Rauch

Alfred B. Weinstein

Assisted by Carole Reynolds

Photo Credits

World of Vocabulary, Purple Level, Third Edition

Sidney J. Rauch • Alfred B. Weinstein

Copyright © 1996 by Globe Fearon Educational Publisher, a division of Paramount Publishing, One Lake Street, Upper Saddle River, New Jersey 07458. All rights reserved. No part of this book may be reproduced or transmitted in any form or by any means, electrical or mechanical, including photocopying, recording, or by any information storage and retrieval system without permission in writing from the publisher.

Printed in the United States of America

3 4 5 6 7 8 9 10   99 98

ISBN 0-8359-1309-0

AUTHORS

*S*idney J. Rauch is Professor Emeritus of Reading and Education at Hofstra University in Hempstead, New York. He has been a visiting professor at numerous universities (University of Vermont; Appalachian State University, North Carolina; Queens College, New York; The State University at Albany, New York) and is active as an author, consultant, and evaluator. His publications include three textbooks, thirty workbooks, and over 80 professional articles. His *World of Vocabulary* series has sold over two and one-half million copies.

Dr. Rauch has served as consultant and/or evaluator for over thirty school districts in New York, Connecticut, Florida, North Carolina, South Carolina, and the U.S. Virgin Islands. His awards include "Reading Educator of the Year" from the New York State Reading Association (1985); "Outstanding Educator Award" presented by the Colby College Alumni Association (1990); and the College Reading Association Award for "Outstanding Contributions to the Field of Reading" (1991). The *Journal of Reading Education* selected Dr. Rauch's article, "The Balancing Effect Continue: Whole Language Faces Reality" for its "Outstanding Article Award," 1993-1994.

Two of the *Barnaby Brown* books, The Visitor from Outer Space, and *The Return of B.B.* were selected as "Children's Choices" winners for 1991 in a poll conducted by the New York State Reading Association.

*A*lfred B. Weinstein is the former principal of Myra S. Barnes Intermediate School (Staten Island, N.Y.). Dr. Weinstein has taught extensively at the secondary school level, and he has served as an elementary school principal and assistant principal. He has been a reading clinician and instructor at Hofstra University Reading Center. At Queens College he gave courses in reading improvement, and at Brooklyn College he taught reading for the New York City Board of Education's in-service teacher training program. He was head of Unit 1 of the Board of Examiners and supervised the licensing of teachers, supervisors, administrators, psychologists, and social workers for the New York City Board of Education. He is vice-president of the Council of Supervisors and Administrators of Local 1 of the AFL-CIO. Dr. Weinstein has been listed in *Who's Who in the East* since 1982.

Dr. Weinstein is a contributor to the Handbook for the Volunteer Tutor and one of the authors of Achieving Reading Skills. With Dr. Rauch, he is coauthor of *Mastering Reading Skills*.

CONTENTS

This was no ordinary opera. The $\boxed{delirious,}$ arm-waving children were watching a musical fantasy called *Where the Wild Things Are*. The "wild things" were monstrous creatures that were 12 feet tall. Their eyes, noses, and horns moved mechanically as they $\boxed{cavorted}$ on the stage, like parts of a giant "animated pop-up book."

These $\boxed{conspicuous}$ creatures were all products of the mind of Maurice Sendak, a talented writer who has written and $\boxed{illustrated}$ more than 80 books, including the award-winning *Where the Wild Things Are* and *In the Night Kitchen*. This creative genius decided to release his characters from the pages of his books and turn them loose upon the stage. There, his memorable $\boxed{vision}$ of childhood came alive.

The "memorable vision" began with Sendak's experiences as a sickly child with a $\boxed{vivid}$ imagination. Sendak $\boxed{collaborated}$ with his brother and sister to create their own books. Jack made up stories, and Natalie $\boxed{constructed}$ the $\boxed{bindings.}$ Sendak drew the pictures on shirt cardboards, never dreaming that this childhood $\boxed{enterprise}$ would be the beginning of a life filled with "wild things." Recently, Sendak created a powerful book about homeless children, titled *We Are All in the Dumps,* with Jack and Guy. Some young readers might consider this book Sendak's most frightening "vision."

UNDERSTANDING THE STORY

>>>> *Circle the letter next to each correct statement.*

1. The statement that best expresses the main idea of this selection is:
   a. Maurice Sendak's vision began in childhood.
   b. Maurice Sendak has designed scenery and costumes and has written words for an opera.
   c. Maurice Sendak is able to transfer his creative ideas into stories and characters for both books and the stage.

2. From this story, you can conclude that
   a. Maurice Sendak is not afraid to take chances with his art.
   b. only children love Maurice Sendak's work.
   c. Sendak's brother and sister are famous in the creative arts.

MAKE AN ALPHABETICAL LIST

>>>> *Here are the ten vocabulary words in this lesson. Write them in alphabetical order in the spaces below.*

constructed	collaborated	cavorted	vivid	enterprise
conspicuous	bindings	illustrated	vision	delirious

1. _____   6. _____

2. _____   7. _____

3. _____   8. _____

4. _____   9. _____

5. _____   10. _____

WHAT DO THE WORDS MEAN?

>>>> *Following are some meanings, or definitions, for the ten vocabulary words in this lesson. Write the words next to their definitions.*

1. _____ worked together; cooperated

2. _____ something imagined, as in a dream

3. _____ ran and jumped around playfully

4. _____ wildly excited; enthusiastic; emotional

5. _____ covers and backings for holding book pages together

6. _____ lively; sharp; clear

7. _____ easily seen; attracting attention

8. _____ a difficult or complicated project

9. _____ built; made

10. _____ created pictures or drawings

4

FIND THE ANALOGIES

>>>> In an **analogy,** similar relationships occur between words that are different. For example, *pig* is to *hog* as *car* is to *automobile*. The relationship is that the words mean the same. Here's another analogy: *noisy* is to *quiet* as *short* is to *tall*. In this relationship, the words have opposite meanings.

>>>> *See if you can complete the following analogies. Circle the correct word.*

1. **Vivid** is to **sharp** as **delirious** is to

   a. bored   b. childish   c. excited   d. controlled

2. **Constructed** is to **destroyed** as **screamed** is to

   a. built   b. whispered   c. yelled   d. convinced

3. **Cavorted** is to **played** as **illustrated** is to

   a. read   b. danced   c. drew   d. explained

4. **Vision** is to **dream** as **bindings** is to

   a. covers   b. reference   c. pages   d. agility

5. **Conspicuous** is to **hidden** as **graceful** is to

   a. religious   b. elegant   c. obvious   d. clumsy

USE YOUR OWN WORDS

>>>> *Look at the picture. What words come into your mind other than the ten vocabulary words used in this lesson? Write them on the lines below. To help you get started, here are two good words:*

1. _____ horns _____
2. _____ stare _____
3. _____
4. _____
5. _____
6. _____
7. _____
8. _____
9. _____
10. _____

IDENTIFY PARTS OF SPEECH

>>>> *The ten vocabulary words in the story represent three different parts of speech. Three of the words are adjectives, four are verbs, and three are nouns. Write each vocabulary word under the part of speech that describes its function.*

Adjectives	Verbs	Nouns
_____	_____	_____
_____	_____	_____
_____	_____	_____
	_____	

COMPLETE THE STORY

>>>> Here are the ten vocabulary words for this lesson:

cavorted	constructed	conspicuous	illustrated	bindings
vivid	vision	delirious	collaborated	enterprise

>>>> *There are seven blank spaces in the story below. Three vocabulary words have already been used in the story. They are underlined. Use the other seven words to fill in the blanks.*

As a child, Maurice Sendak <u>collaborated</u> with Jack and Natalie in their own little workshop. While others _____, Sendak, a sickly boy, developed his art. He loved writing and drawing <u>vivid</u> pictures of his unique _____.

Sendak welcomed the chance to release his <u>conspicuous</u> characters onto the stage. For him, this would be a new and exciting _____. These creatures were _____ to look like the monsters he had _____ in his book.

Sendak's monstrous creatures seemed thrilled to have escaped from their _____. They appeared to come alive and to actually enjoy performing before _____ audiences everywhere.

Learn More About Fantasy

>>>> *On a separate piece of paper or in your notebook or journal, complete one or more of the activities below.*

Working Together

Get a copy of *Where the Wild Things Are*. With your group, plan how to turn this book into a play for children. Plan the dialogue, sets, costumes, lights, actors, direction, and production of the play. Practice your play. Then perform it for a group of children.

Learning Across the Curriculum

Why do children have nightmares, play make-believe, or have imaginary friends? Find out what researchers have discovered about how children think and write an explanation.

Broadening Your Understanding

Read several of Sendak's books to understand the fantastic world about which he writes. Then write your own book of fantasy for children. Draw your own illustrations or cut them out of magazines and create a book. Show it to a child you know to see if he or she understands and enjoys it.

2 THE GREAT GRETZKY

Ask anyone in the National Hockey League, "Who is the $\boxed{dominant}$ player in the game?" The answer will most like be "Wayne Gretzky." There will be little debate about the choice. Gretzky is rewriting the record books. In 1989, he became the greatest scorer in NHL history. He had already $\boxed{eclipsed}$ most scoring records, but he set a new one when he $\boxed{toppled}$ Gordie Howe's record of 1,850 points. This achievement was once thought to be an $\boxed{unattainable}$ goal. Gretzky has made the record book look $\boxed{obsolete.}$

Who is this young wonder whose name is being mentioned in the same breath with Gordie Howe and Bobby Orr? Gretzky is the frontline center of the Los Angeles Kings. He is the $\boxed{focus}$ of all eyes when he steps on the ice. He has such $\boxed{fantastic}$ talent and intelligence that both teammates and opponents have great respect for him. When Gretzky $\boxed{bombards}$ the net or passes to a teammate, the opposing team is taken by surprise. Their $\boxed{facial}$ expressions seem to say, "Impossible!" His teammates, however, are $\boxed{jubilant.}$ His play seems to inspire them to greater efforts. One example is the 1993 season. Gretzky missed the first half because of back problems. He returned to the team and became the leading scorer in the playoffs, making three goals in one game.

Gretzky's skill and fame have made him a national hero and a very rich person. He is paid millions of dollars for pushing a puck, but no one does it with the speed and control of the Great Gretzky.

UNDERSTANDING THE STORY

>>>> *Circle the letter next to each correct statement.*

1. The statement that best expresses the main idea of this selection is:
   a. Only once in a decade does a player of Gretzky's ability come along.
   b. Wayne Gretzky has a long way to go before he can be compared to Gordie Howe.
   c. Wayne Gretzky is one among many good players in the National Hockey League.

2. The statement, "Gretzky has made the record books look obsolete," means that
   a. the record book is out of date and should be revised.
   b. records are being broken at a very fast rate by this amazing young man.
   c. Gretzky should have a record book for his own personal scoring records.

MAKE AN ALPHABETICAL LIST

>>>> *Here are the ten vocabulary words in this lesson. Write them in alphabetical order in the spaces below.*

focus	toppled	fantastic	unattainable	dominant
jubilant	obsolete	facial	eclipsed	bombards

1. _____   6. _____

2. _____   7. _____

3. _____   8. _____

4. _____   9. _____

5. _____   10. _____

WHAT DO THE WORDS MEAN?

>>>> *Following are some meanings, or definitions, for the ten vocabulary words in this lesson. Write the words next to their definitions.*

1. _____ attacks strongly

2. _____ filled with great joy; extremely happy

3. _____ overthrown; pushed over

4. _____ no longer in use; out of fashion

5. _____ of or relating to the face

6. _____ went beyond; overshadowed

7. _____ commanding

8. _____ out of reach

9. _____ the center of attention

10. _____ unbelievable; amazing

FIND THE ANALOGIES

>>>> In an **analogy,** similar relationships occur between words that are different. For example, *pig* is to *hog* as *car* is to *automobile*. The relationship is that the words mean the same. Here's another analogy: *noisy* is to *quiet* as *short* is to *tall*. In this relationship, the words have opposite meanings.

>>>> *See if you can complete the following analogies. Circle the correct word or words.*

1. **Toppled** is to **erected** as **destroyed** is to

   a. created   b. wiped out   c. terrorized   d. criticized

2. **Jubilant** is to **happy** as **unattainable** is to

   a. unorganized   b. unreachable   c. uninspired   d. ordinary

3. **Dominant** is to **superior** as **fantastic** is to

   a. fearful   b. usual   c. amazing   d. ordinary

4. **Eclipsed** is to **surpassed** as **bombards** is to

   a. attacks   b. retreats   c. destroys   d. overthrows

5. **Focus** is to **center** as **consumer** is to

   a. employer   b. assistant   c. buyer   d. traveler

USE YOUR OWN WORDS

>>>> *Look at the picture. What words come into your mind other than the ten vocabulary words used in this lesson? Write them on the lines below. To help you get started, here are two good words:*

1. _____ competition _____
2. _____ movement _____
3. _____
4. _____
5. _____
6. _____
7. _____
8. _____
9. _____
10. _____

IDENTIFY PARTS OF SPEECH

>>>> The ten vocabulary words in the story represent three different parts of speech. Six of the words are adjectives, three are verbs, and one is a noun. Write each vocabulary word under the part of speech that describes its function.

Adjectives	Verbs	Noun
_____	_____	_____
_____	_____	
_____	_____	
_____		
_____		
_____		

COMPLETE THE STORY

>>>> Here are the ten vocabulary words for this lesson:

focus	obsolete	fantastic	unattainable	facial
jubilant	bombards	toppled	eclipsed	dominant

>>>> *There are seven blank spaces in the story below. Three vocabulary words have already been used in the story. They are underlined. Use the other seven words to fill in the blanks.*

A player with Wayne Gretzky's talents comes along once in a decade. He is such a _____ figure that the sportswriters have already used up their synonyms for "great." The Los Angeles Kings are _____ because this <u>fantastic</u> player is on their team. He has _____ one record after another. To date, he has <u>eclipsed</u> 22 league records and has made them <u>obsolete</u>. His latest record was scoring a point or more in 30 straight games.

In practically every game, Gretzky is the _____ of all eyes. Fans expect him to score, no matter how tough the opposition. Rarely does Gretzky disappoint them. He _____ the net with hard, accurate shots. Some of the shots are so unbelievable that the _____ expressions of the other players show their amazement. The way he has broken scoring records that were once considered _____ has made him a wonder in hockey history. Because he is still a very young man, one doesn't know how really good he can be! It's difficult to imagine his becoming any better.

Learn More About Professional Sports

>>>> *On a separate piece of paper or in your notebook or journal, complete one or more of the activities below.*

Broadening Your Understanding

Look up the names of hockey teams or other sports teams. Find out how they got their names and write a paragraph about it.

Learning Across the Curriculum

Who first played hockey? How has the sport changed? Write a short history of the game. Illustrate your report with pictures of old-time hockey players.

Broadening Your Understanding

Do athletes deserve the huge amounts of money some are paid? Take one side of the debate while a partner takes the other side. Research arguments for your side. Have a debate before the class. After the debate, see who managed to convince the class of her or his argument.

3 CONQUERING DRAGONS

Laurence Yep, author of *Dragonwings, Child of the Owl,* and many other popular novels, was born in San Francisco, California, on June 14, 1948. As a child, he thought of himself only as an American. Once, after watching old cartoons about Chinese laundrymen, he pulled his eyes into a slant and ran around copying the high-pitched noises the laundrymen made. His mother watched him in disbelief. "You're Chinese!" she chided. "Stop that!"

As a child, Yep had no desire to be Chinese and managed to sit through Chinese classes without absorbing a word of the language. As he grew older, Yep changed his mind. He remembers venturing into San Francisco's Chinatown to learn how to be Chinese. He also learned about his culture from his Chinese grandmother who lived in Brooklyn, New York.

However, Yep was too American to fit into Chinatown and too Chinese to feel truly comfortable anywhere else. An unathletic child in an athletic family, Yep felt disconnected from just about everyone. He perceived life as a frustrating puzzle until he discovered his flair for writing.

Yep admits that when he writes about aliens in his science fiction, he is writing about himself as a Chinese American. He says he is indebted to his memories of his youth and uses them as assets, working bits and pieces of his life into his stories. His research into Chinatown and Chinese immigrants has helped him appreciate his own background and nationality. At the same time, his irresistible stories of dragons and heroes captivate thousands of eager readers.

UNDERSTANDING THE STORY

>>>> *Circle the letter next to each correct statement.*

1. The statement that best expresses the main idea of this selection is:
   a. As a child, Laurence Yep did not realize he was Chinese.
   b. As a child, Yep wanted to watch old movies.
   c. Yep's books are greatly influenced by his childhood memories and his feelings as a Chinese American.

2. From this story, you can conclude that
   a. Laurence Yep experienced discrimination because of his Chinese background.
   b. Yep now has considerable pride in his cultural background.
   c. learning to speak Chinese helped Yep appreciate his background.

15

MAKE AN ALPHABETICAL LIST

>>>> *Here are the ten vocabulary words in this lesson. Write them in alphabetical order in the spaces below.*

indebted	perceived	captivate	irresistible	disbelief
flair	chided	assets	disconnected	nationality

1. _____

2. _____

3. _____

4. _____

5. _____

6. _____

7. _____

8. _____

9. _____

10. _____

WHAT DO THE WORDS MEAN?

>>>> *Following are some meanings, or definitions, for the ten vocabulary words in this lesson. Write the words next to their definitions.*

1. _____ owing something to someone

2. _____ to charm; to capture someone's interest

3. _____ understood

4. _____ a skill or talent

5. _____ having a strong appeal or attraction

6. _____ resources; advantages

7. _____ separated

8. _____ spoke out in anger or disapproval

9. _____ rejection of something as untrue

10. _____ membership in the cultural group of a particular nation

FIND THE ANALOGIES

>>>> In an **analogy,** the relationship between one pair of words is the same as the relationship between another pair of words. For example, here is one kind of analogy: *dog* is to *friendly* as *feeling* is to *uncomfortable*. In this relationship, the first word in each pair is an object or idea, and the second word in each pair describes the object or idea.

>>>> *See if you can complete the following analogies. Circle the correct word.*

1. **Grandmother** is to **comforting** as **flair** is to

   a. skirt   b. artistic   c. relative   d. family

2. **Patient** is to **ailing** as **assets** are to

   a. extensive   b. sick   c. liable   d. disconnected

3. **Nationality** is to **perceived** as **memories** are to

   a. culture   b. discrimination   c. recalled   d. brain

4. **Disbelief** is to **shocked** as **ancestor** is to

   a. chided   b. culture   c. admired   d. generation

USE YOUR OWN WORDS

>>>> *Look at the picture. What words come into your mind other than the ten vocabulary words used in this lesson? Write them on the lines below. To help you get started, here are two good words:*

1. _____ mountains _____
2. _____ dragons _____
3. _____
4. _____
5. _____
6. _____
7. _____
8. _____
9. _____
10. _____

MAKE NEW WORDS FROM OLD

>>>> *Look at the vocabulary word below. See how many words you can form by using the letters of this word. Think of at least nine words. One has already been done for you. Write your words in the spaces below.*

nationality

1. _____ nation _____   6._____

2. _____   7._____

3. _____   8._____

4. _____   9._____

5. _____   10._____

COMPLETE THE STORY

>>>> Here are the ten vocabulary words for this lesson:

disconnected	indebted	perceived	chided	irresistible
assets	nationality	disbelief	flair	captivate

>>>> *There are seven blank spaces in the story below. Three vocabulary words have already been used in the story. They are underlined. Use the other seven words to fill in the blanks.*

Many readers may feel _____ when they hear that Laurence Yep at one time rejected his Chinese _____. He recalls the time his mother _____ him for pretending to be Chinese. Yep now says he is _____ to a background that has enabled him to create such _____ stories. He now knows his culture is one of his many _____, along with his natural <u>flair</u> for writing. The Chinese influence in his stories helps to <u>captivate</u> readers. Yep's experience may help assure readers who feel _____ from their own families. What he <u>perceived</u> as a child is not what he perceives as an adult.

Learn More About Writing

>>>> *On a separate piece of paper or in your notebook or journal, complete one or more of the activities below.*

Learning Across the Curriculum

Write a short story that includes an event or character from your childhood. Share your story with a partner or small group.

Broadening Your Understanding

Research the background of Yoshiko Uchida, Ed Young, or another Asian American writer. Find out how the author uses childhood experiences in his or her work. Share your information with the class.

Extending Your Reading

Read one or more of Laurence Yep's books listed below or read his autobiography *The Lost Garden*. Explain how you think the story might have been influenced by the author's childhood feelings of being disconnected from others.

Dragonwings
Child of the Owl
Sea Glass
Sweetwater
Kind Hearts and Gentle Monsters
Dragon of the Lost Sea
Dragon Steel
Dragon Cauldron
Dragon War

4 A JUSTICE FOR ALL

The Supreme Court has been in ☐*existence*☐ for more than 200 years. It had consisted only of male judges until 1982, when Sandra Day O'Connor was ☐*unanimously*☐ elected to be the first woman justice of the Supreme Court.

O'Connor was born in Arizona on the family ranch. Even in early childhood, she loved horses. She ☐*groomed*☐ and rode them. She never had to ☐*overcome*☐ the fears some of her friends had about riding. They felt ☐*inadequate*☐ when it came to handling horses, but O'Connor was at home with these magnificent animals.

O'Connor discovered her love for the law at Stanford University. She later married and ☐*resided*☐ in Arizona. There, O'Connor entered ☐*Republican*☐ politics. She was elected to the Arizona State Senate. O'Connor then moved up to become its majority leader.

With her experience, it seemed only natural that the Republican Party should ask her to run for governor. O'Connor turned down the offer. She preferred to become a judge on the U.S. Court of Appeals. Her reputation there was that of a no-nonsense judge. O'Connor gave out strict prison sentences. She was an ☐*exception*☐ among judges.

In 1982, President Ronald Reagan needed a justice to fill a Supreme Court ☐*vacancy.*☐ He appointed three committees to search throughout the country. O'Connor's name was on each committee's list. For days, she underwent ☐*harsh*☐ questioning by the Senate. She was found to be highly qualified. When President Reagan finally appointed Sandra Day O'Connor to the Supreme Court, he said she was "a person for all seasons."

UNDERSTANDING THE STORY

>>>> *Circle the letter next to each correct statement.*

1. The statement that best expresses the main idea of this selection is:
   a. Supreme Court judges are selected for political reasons.
   b. Sandra Day O'Connor enjoyed the law more than politics.
   c. Determination and hard work helped Sandra Day O'Connor get where she is today.

2. When President Reagan called Justice O'Connor "a person for all seasons," he meant that
   a. she is the kind of person who could handle all problems with intelligence.
   b. she would fit in well with other judges on the Supreme Court.
   c. she would not allow the Senate to stop her from working.

MAKE AN ALPHABETICAL LIST

>>>> *Here are the ten vocabulary words in this lesson. Write them in alphabetical order in the spaces below.*

existence	unanimously	vacancy	harsh	exception
Republican	resided	overcome	inadequate	groomed

1. _____
2. _____
3. _____
4. _____
5. _____

6. _____
7. _____
8. _____
9. _____
10. _____

WHAT DO THE WORDS MEAN?

>>>> *Following are some meanings, or definitions, for the ten vocabulary words in this lesson. Write the words next to their definitions.*

1. _____ one of the two major U.S. political parties

2. _____ severe; sometimes even hostile

3. _____ lived; dwelled

4. _____ undisputedly

5. _____ an empty space; an opening

6. _____ combed and brushed; rubbed down

7. _____ not good enough; lacking; below par

8. _____ life; being

9. _____ to defeat; to get the better of

10. _____ different; one of a kind

FIND THE ANALOGIES

>>>> In an **analogy,** similar relationships occur between words that are different. For example, *pig* is to *hog* as *car* is to *automobile*. The relationship is that the words mean the same. Here's another analogy: *noisy* is to *quiet* as *short* is to *tall*. In this relationship, the words have opposite meanings.

>>>> *See if you can complete the following analogies. Circle the correct word.*

1. **Inadequate** is to **powerless** as **persistent** is to

    a. harmful   b. unyielding   c. permissive   d. powerful

2. **Harsh** is to **gentle** as **uncertain** is to

    a. positive   b. clear   c. peculiar   d. false

3. **Vacancy** is to **opening** as **arrival** is to

    a. appearance   b. denial   c. defeat   d. departure

4. **Existence** is to **death** as **exception** is to

    a. excellence   b. omission   c. uniformity   d. fairness

5. **Resided** is to **wandered** as **admired** is to

    a. decided   b. liked   c. disliked   d. followed

USE YOUR OWN WORDS

>>>> *Look at the picture. What words come into your mind other than the ten vocabulary words used in this lesson? Write them on the lines below. To help you get started, here are two good words:*

1.   robed

2.   proud

3. _____

4. _____

5. _____

6. _____

7. _____

8. _____

9. _____

10. _____

FIND THE ADJECTIVES

>>>> An **adjective** is a word that modifies or describes a noun (the name of a person, place, or thing). The adjectives are underlined in the following examples: The <u>small</u> boy cried; the <u>old</u> truck stalled; he ran to the <u>haunted</u> house.

>>>> *Underline all of the adjectives in the sentences below.*

1. O'Connor had a difficult time when she groomed the brown stallion.

2. Sandra Day O'Connor is a strict judge.

3. O'Connor had a carefree, enjoyable life on her parents' ranch.

4. The Senate felt O'Connor was a fair, intelligent judge, so they unanimously voted for her.

5. Sandra Day O'Connor behaved in a cool, calm manner when she answered the harsh questions put to her by the senators.

COMPLETE THE STORY

>>>> Here are the ten vocabulary words for this lesson:

exception	existence	inadequate	groomed	overcome
harsh	Republican	resided	unanimously	vacancy

>>>> *There are seven blank spaces in the story below. Three vocabulary words have already been used in the story. They are underlined. Use the other seven words to fill in the blanks.*

As a child, O'Connor _____ horses on her parents' ranch. Unlike her friends, she never felt _____ around these animals. Her friends couldn't _____ their fears around horses. O'Connor was the <u>exception</u>.

When O'Connor became a lawyer, she joined the _____ party in Arizona where she _____. She was such a fine judge that President Reagan recommended that she be chosen to fill the _____ on the Supreme Court, making her the first woman justice in the Supreme Court's <u>existence</u>. After asking extremely <u>harsh</u> questions, the Senate voted for her _____.

Learn More About the Supreme Court

>>>> *On a separate piece of paper or in your notebook or journal, complete one or more of the activities below.*

Learning Across the Curriculum

Research the history of the Supreme Court decision in the case *Brown* v. *Board of Education of Topeka, Kansas*. Find out what the issues were, the arguments of both sides, and what the Supreme Court decided. Write how you think this decision has influenced the country.

Broadening Your Understanding

How does someone become a Supreme Court justice? Find out the requirements for becoming a justice. Look at some of the people who have become judges on the Supreme Court. Write a strategy for how a person could plan a career, hoping to become a Supreme Court judge.

Extending Your Reading

Read one of the following books about people who became judges on the Supreme Court. Report on the important rulings one of the Supreme Court justices made in his or her career.

Great Justices of the Supreme Court, by Nathan Aaseng
Sandra Day O'Connor, by Norman Macht
Thurgood Marshall, by Lisa Aldred

5 MAN WITH A DREAM

Stephen Hawking is a *celebrated* scientist. He has been called the most brilliant *theoretical* *physicist* since Albert Einstein. He has spent his life trying to understand how the universe began. He believes he is now closer than ever to reaching that understanding. He is searching for the grand *unification* theory to explain the link between the forces that affect the large bodies of the universe and the forces that affect *particles* smaller than atoms. Hawking thinks this link is the key to learning how the universe came into being.

Hawking is thought to be an *astonishing* man because of his brilliant mind. He is even more exceptional, however, because he does his work while suffering from an *incurable* disease known as Lou Gehrig's disease. He is paralyzed and unable to speak. He is *confined* to a wheelchair.

Hawking can make only one movement, a barely *perceptible* twitch of his fingers. He communicates with the world by using a specially designed computer that can be operated by that one movement. Hawking uses his computer both to write and to speak.

Although Hawking is *dependent* on both his wheelchair and his computer, he writes books, teaches classes, and travels around the world to meet other scientists. He even made a guest appearance as himself on "Star Trek: The Next Generation." Hawking says the reason for his work is very simple. "My goal," he says, "is a complete understanding of the universe."

UNDERSTANDING THE STORY

>>>> *Circle the letter next to each correct statement.*

1. The statement that best expresses the main idea of this selection is:
   a. Lou Gehrig's disease is an incurable disease.
   b. Stephen Hawking is a brilliant theoretical physicist despite his being paralyzed and unable to speak.
   c. The grand unification theory will explain how the world began.

2. From this story, you can conclude that
   a. scientists all agree on how the universe came into being.
   b. Stephen Hawking is confined to his bed.
   c. Stephen Hawking is a courageous man.

MAKE AN ALPHABETICAL LIST

>>>> *Here are the ten vocabulary words in this lesson. Write them in alphabetical order in the spaces below.*

particles	incurable	theoretical	perceptible	celebrated
dependent	physicist	unification	astonishing	confined

1. _____   6. _____

2. _____   7. _____

3. _____   8. _____

4. _____   9. _____

5. _____   10. _____

WHAT DO THE WORDS MEAN?

>>>> *Following are some meanings, or definitions, for the ten vocabulary words in this lesson. Write the words next to their definitions.*

1. _____ minute pieces of matter

2. _____ restricted to a particular place

3. _____ amazing; surprising

4. _____ the bringing together of; consolidation

5. _____ concerned principally with abstractions and theories

6. _____ not able to be healed or cured

7. _____ famous; renowned

8. _____ capable of being seen or noticed

9. _____ to be reliant on other people or things for what is needed

10. _____ an expert in the science that deals with matter and energy

FIND THE ANALOGIES

>>>> In an **analogy,** similar relationships occur between words that are different. For example, *pig* is to *hog* as *car* is to *automobile*. The relationship is that the words mean the same. Here's another analogy: *noisy* is to *quiet* as *short* is to *tall*. In this relationship, the words have opposite meanings.

>>>> *See if you can complete the following analogies. Circle the correct word or words.*

1. **Dependent** is to **independent** as **probable** is to

    a. necessary   b. promising   c. unlikely   d. unjust

2. **Confined** is to **restrained** as **awkward** is to

    a. ungraceful   b. agile   c. quick   d. nimble

3. **Perceptible** is to **noticeable** as **arid** is to

    a. moist   b. wet   c. deserted   d. dry

4. **Celebrated** is to **renowned** as **unique** is to

    a. truthful   b. lonely   c. special   d. same

5. **Physicist** is to **scientist** as **daffodil** is to

    a. yellow   b. flower   c. tree   d. smell

USE YOUR OWN WORDS

>>>> *Look at the picture. What words come into your mind other than the ten vocabulary words used in this lesson? Write them on the lines below. To help you get started, here are two good words:*

1.   wheelchair
2.   scholarly
3.   _____
4.   _____
5.   _____
6.   _____
7.   _____
8.   _____
9.   _____
10.   _____

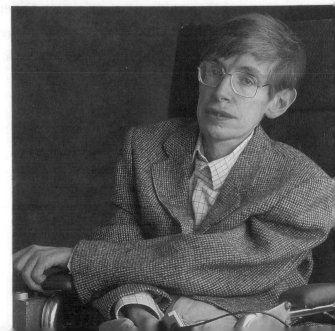

MATCH THE ANTONYMS

>>>> **Antonyms** are words that are opposite in meaning. For example, *good* and *bad* and *heavy* and *light* are antonyms.

>>>> *Match the vocabulary words on the left with the antonyms on the right. Write the correct letter in the space.*

Vocabulary Words	Antonyms
1. _____ incurable	**a.** common
2. _____ particles	**b.** practical
3. _____ perceptible	**c.** separation
4. _____ celebrated	**d.** unseen
5. _____ unification	**e.** curable
6. _____ astonishing	**f.** wholes
7. _____ theoretical	**g.** unknown

COMPLETE THE STORY

>>>> Here are the ten vocabulary words for this lesson:

dependent	incurable	astonishing	celebrated	physicist
confined	unification	particles	perceptible	theoretical

>>>> *There are seven blank spaces in the story below. Three vocabulary words have already been used in the story. They are underlined. Use the other seven words to fill in the blanks.*

Stephen Hawking may be _____ to a wheelchair, but he is still one of the world's most <u>celebrated</u> scientists. Having an _____ disease has not stopped Hawking from pursuing his life's work—developing his grand _____ theory. As a <u>theoretical</u> _____, Hawking studies the sun and the planets, as well as _____ smaller than atoms.

Although Hawking is paralyzed and cannot speak, he is able to communicate with other people through the use of a special computer. Hawking is <u>dependent</u> on the computer for both writing and speaking. He operates the machine by a twitch of his fingers that is barely _____. It is an _____ machine. With its help, Hawking can continue his search for an understanding of how the universe began.

30

Learn More About Scientists

>>>> *On a separate piece of paper or in your notebook or journal, complete one or more of the activities below.*

Learning Across the Curriculum

Even though few people can understand all of Stephen Hawking's ideas, many can understand the basis for theories about how the universe began. Research some of these theories. Describe the one that makes the most sense to you. Explain why the theory seems most practical or realistic to you.

Broadening Your Understanding

Scientists work in many fields, such as physics, botany, psychology, zoology, and chemistry. Research a field of science that interests you. Find out what a scientist in that field does. What is his or her life like? Share what you discover with the class in an oral presentation.

Extending Your Reading

Scientists, such as the ones written about in the books below, have had an enormous impact on the world. Read one of these books and explain how the world would be different without the discoveries made by this person.

Benjamin Franklin, by Eve Feldman
Albert Einstein, by Karin Ireland
Galileo, by Leonard Everett Fisher
George Washington, by Richard Tames

6 LIFE IN THE THEATER

The booming, $\boxed{\textit{mellifluous}}$ voice of Othello fills the stage. Its power $\boxed{\textit{envelops}}$ the spellbound audience. The curtain falls to loud applause. James Earl Jones, a towering actor, receives a standing ovation. This is the first time he has played Othello on Broadway. The New York critics $\boxed{\textit{raved}}$ about his performance.

Jones played in the Broadway play *Fences* and won a Tony Award for Best Actor. The $\boxed{\textit{forbidding}}$ figure of Darth Vader in *Star Wars* owed its strength to Jones's rich voice. So did King Mufasa, Simba's father, in *The Lion King*. He also co-starred in the popular film *Field of Dreams*. He also received worldwide recognition for his role in *Roots*.

The road to success was not smooth. Jones stuttered as a child and was $\boxed{\textit{mute}}$ in school. To encourage him to speak, a high school English teacher $\boxed{\textit{prescribed}}$ a program of voice lessons and public speaking. Jones had to $\boxed{\textit{utilize}}$ his voice to overcome his speaking problem. In college, he switched from medicine to acting. When he enrolled in The American Theater Wing, he was a $\boxed{\textit{convert}}$ to acting.

Jones was raised by his grandparents. The imaginative tales his grandmother told him strengthened his $\boxed{\textit{dramatic}}$ sense. His father, also an actor, helped him prepare for the role of Shakespeare's Othello. He $\boxed{\textit{emphasized}}$ the need to show Othello's nobility. Jones studies all of the characters he plays in great detail and believes that an actor must keep on acting or he will be forgotten. There seems to be little chance of James Earl Jones ever being forgotten.

UNDERSTANDING THE STORY

>>>> *Circle the letter next to each correct statement.*

1. The statement that best expresses the main idea of this selection is:
   a. Since he was a young child, James Earl Jones wanted to be an actor.
   b. Dedication, dramatic talent, and a marvelous voice helped James Earl Jones become a great actor.
   c. Because he stuttered as a child, James Earl Jones achieved acting success.

2. From this story, you can conclude that
   a. Jones will begin to write plays for Broadway.
   b. Jones will continue acting to maintain his reputation and strengthen his dramatic ability.
   c. Jones will purchase a theater to help struggling actors learn their craft.

MAKE AN ALPHABETICAL LIST

>>>> *Here are the ten vocabulary words in this lesson. Write them in alphabetical order in the spaces below.*

raved	envelops	emphasized	prescribed	utilize
forbidding	mute	convert	dramatic	mellifluous

1. _____

2. _____

3. _____

4. _____

5. _____

6. _____

7. _____

8. _____

9. _____

10. _____

WHAT DO THE WORDS MEAN?

>>>> *Following are some meanings, or definitions, for the ten vocabulary words in this lesson. Write the words next to their definitions.*

1. _____ a new believer; a new follower

2. _____ to use; to employ

3. _____ unable to speak; silent

4. _____ surrounds; wraps around

5. _____ theatrical; describing acting ability

6. _____ frightening; fearful

7. _____ stressed; made important

8. _____ praised highly

9. _____ musical; flowing

10. _____ urged; strongly advised; recommended

FIND THE ANALOGIES

>>>> In an **analogy,** similar relationships occur between words that are different. For example, *pig* is to *hog* as *car* is to *automobile*. The relationship is that the words mean the same. Here's another analogy: *noisy* is to *quiet* as *short* is to *tall*. In this relationship, the words have opposite meanings.

>>>> *See if you can complete the following analogies. Circle the correct word.*

1. **Mute** is to **silent** as **talkative** is to

   a. gossipy   b. thoughtful   c. needy   d. contrary

2. **Raved** is to **disapproved** as **repelled** is to

   a. repeated   b. attracted   c. rejected   d. recalled

3. **Prescribed** is to **recommended** as **received** is to

   a. gotten   b. shared   c. improved   d. left

4. **Dramatic** is to **theatrical** as **mellifluous** is to

   a. painful   b. musical   c. limber   d. practical

5. **Convert** is to **unbeliever** as **emphasis** is to

   a. stress   b. indifference   c. accent   d. conduct

USE YOUR OWN WORDS

>>>> *Look at the picture. What words come into your mind other than the ten vocabulary words used in this lesson? Write them on the lines below. To help you get started, here are two good words:*

1. _____impressive_____
2. _____stare_____
3. _____
4. _____
5. _____
6. _____
7. _____
8. _____
9. _____
10. _____

MAKE NEW WORDS FROM OLD

>>>> **Look at the vocabulary word below. See how many words you can form by using the letters of this word. Think of at least 11 words. One has already been done for you. Write your words in the spaces below.**

emphasized

1. _____size_____   7. _____
2. _____   8. _____
3. _____   9. _____
4. _____   10. _____
5. _____   11. _____
6. _____   12. _____

COMPLETE THE STORY

>>>> Here are the ten vocabulary words for this lesson:

mellifluous	utilize	prescribed	envelops	forbidding
dramatic	emphasized	convert	raved	mute

>>>> **There are seven blank spaces in the story below. Three vocabulary words have already been used in the story. They are underlined. Use the other seven words to fill in the blanks.**

James Earl Jones possesses a _____ voice. He is a commanding figure on the stage. His _____ ability to portray a character is obvious in his role as Othello. Jones's father _____ certain qualities in the role for Jones to work on to be effective. Jones <u>envelops</u> the entire audience in the play through his dramatic manner and strong voice. Critics _____ about his performance.

Originally, Jones thought he would be a doctor. But a taste for acting made him a <u>convert</u> to the theater.

When he was in high school, he had trouble speaking in public. He was _____ for a time and didn't know how to deal with it. Lucikly, his English teacher <u>prescribed</u> voice exercises for him. He learned from this teacher and other dramatic coaches how to _____ his voice in the theater. His voice is so magnificient that he was chosen to speak the part of Darth Vader, the _____ villain in *Star Wars*.

Learn More About Working as an Actor

>>>> *On a separate piece of paper or in your notebook or journal, complete one or more of the activities below.*

Appreciating Diversity

There are famous plays in every language. Find a play in your native language and summarize it in English. Then think about the play. Would it appeal to English speakers? Why or why not?

Broadening Your Understanding

James Earl Jones's voice is in such demand that he could make a good living just doing voice-overs. A voice-over occurs when an actor is heard but not seen. Listen to several TV commercials that have voice-overs. Analyze and write why the person making a commercial used that kind of voice to sell that product. Then write whether you think the voice-over is successful in helping to make the point the commercial wants to make.

Extending Your Reading

Read one of the plays in the following books. Then choose one of the main characters in the play. Look at the role as if you were the actor playing it. Explain how you would play the character. How would you look? How would you use your voice? How would you move on the stage?

A Treasury of the Theatre, edited by John Gassner
The Big Book of Comedies, edited by Sylvia E. Kamerman
Best Short Plays, edited by Stanley Richards
24 Favorite One-Act Plays, edited by Bennett Cerf

7 FIGHTING WORDS

"We defended our country with our language," says one of the 400 Navajos who became code talkers during World War II. The marines recruited Navajo males as young as 15 years old from their reservations in Arizona and New Mexico. They wanted people who were $\boxed{articulate}$ in the Navajo language. These Native Americans worked in teams to help direct U.S. troop operations in the Pacific. They relayed messages to each other in Navajo, which only they could understand.

Before the code talkers, the Japanese had quickly broken codes used by the United States. They easily translated messages from command centers to $\boxed{infantry}$ in the field. Because the Japanese knew every move the United States planned, the entire U.S. war operation was at risk. However, messages relayed in the complex Navajo language $\boxed{thwarted}$ the Japanese, who were unable to break them. The Navajo code talkers soon became $\boxed{indispensable}$ members of the marines.

Besides $\boxed{legitimate}$ Navajo words, the code talkers devised new ones. For example, "besh-lo," meaning "iron fish," was used for *submarine*. In all, Navajo communication $\boxed{specialists}$ created 411 new terms. The Japanese were unable to decipher any of them. Even other Americans thought the messages were $\boxed{random}$ sounds.

At Iwo Jima, code talkers sent and received more than 800 messages. They relayed urgent $\boxed{data}$ from $\boxed{platoons}$ on the front lines to command centers. Their skill and dedication helped to win that battle and $\boxed{avert}$ many American deaths.

There is a sculpture in Phoenix, Arizona, of a young Navajo that, along with many other tributes, honors the Navajo code talkers.

UNDERSTANDING THE STORY

>>>> *Circle the letter next to each correct statement.*

1. The statement that best expresses the main idea of this selection is:
   a. Being a code talker required considerable courage.
   b. Code talkers used their native language to help win the war.
   c. The Japanese did not realize Native Americans were members of the marines.

2. From this story, you can conclude that
   a. the Japanese were not familiar with the Navajo language.
   b. the United States will use Navajo code talkers in future wars.
   c. code talkers were given special privileges because of their skills.

MAKE AN ALPHABETICAL LIST

>>>> *Here are the ten vocabulary words in this lesson. Write them in alphabetical order in the spaces below.*

specialists	platoons	data	legitimate	indispensable
thwarted	articulate	avert	random	infantry

1. _____

2. _____

3. _____

4. _____

5. _____

6. _____

7. _____

8. _____

9. _____

10. _____

WHAT DO THE WORDS MEAN?

>>>> *Following are some meanings, or definitions, for the ten vocabulary words in this lesson. Write the words next to their definitions.*

1. _____ having no clear pattern

2. _____ skilled in using language

3. _____ to prevent something from happening; to avoid

4. _____ divisions of a military unit

5. _____ information

6. _____ essential; absolutely necessary

7. _____ soldiers who fight on foot

8. _____ baffled or opposed effectively

9. _____ people who have special training

10. _____ not false; legal; justified

FIND THE ANALOGIES

>>>> In an **analogy,** the relationship between one pair of words is the same as the relationship between another pair of words. For example, here is one kind of analogy: *slice* is to *pie* as *student* is to *class*. In this relationship, the first word in each pair is part of the second word in each pair.

>>>> *See if you can complete the following analogies. Circle the correct word or words.*

1. **Page** is to **book** as **number** is to

   a. paper   b. data   c. legitimate   d. proven

2. **Citizen** is to **nation** as **soldier** is to

   a. infantry   b. voter   c. rifle   d. sergeant

3. **Specialist** is to **army** as **bookkeeper** is to

   a. data   b. infantry   c. company   d. indispensable

4. **Platoon** is to **infantry** as **Air Force** is to

   a. staff   b. worker   c. armed services   d. training

USE YOUR OWN WORDS

>>>> *Look at the picture. What words come into your mind other than the ten vocabulary words used in this lesson? Write them on the lines below. To help you get started, here are two good words:*

1. _____communication_____
2. _____responsibility_____
3. _____
4. _____
5. _____
6. _____
7. _____
8. _____
9. _____
10. _____

USE ANOTHER FORM OF THE WORD

>>>> One word can have several different forms. For example, *act* is a verb, *action* is a noun, *active* is an adjective, and *actively* is an adverb. The correct form of the word depends on its use in the sentence.

>>>> *Complete each sentence below by writing in the correct form of the word at the end of the sentence.*

1. The code talkers were _____ recruited into the infantry. (quick)

2. They were _____ in the Navajo language. (articulation)

3. Teams of Navajo code _____ talked to each other. (specialty)

4. The data they were sent was _____. (secretly)

5. The Navajos _____ their country with their language. (defense)

COMPLETE THE STORY

>>>> Here are the ten vocabulary words for this lesson:

infantry	random	thwarted	articulate	indispensable
platoons	specialists	avert	data	legitimate

>>>> *There are seven blank spaces in the story below. Three vocabulary words have already been used in the story. They are underlined. Use the other seven words to fill in the blanks.*

In order to _____ defeat by the Japanese, the Marines searched for people who were _____ in a language the Japanese would not understand. The Navajo's complex language _____ the Japanese code _____. The Japanese might have thought messages in Navaj were _____ sounds, not <u>legitimate</u> words. Using their unique language, Navajo code talkers were able to send secret _____ to <u>infantry</u> at the front lines. This <u>indispensable</u> information enabled _____ to change their positions without detection by the Japanese.

Learn More About Codes

>>>> *On a separate piece of paper or in your notebook or journal, complete one or more of the activities below.*

Building Language

There are many kinds of codes that do not rely on speech. Research one of them, such as sign language for the hearing impaired or sign language from Native Americans. Then give an oral presentation. If you can, demonstrate the sign language.

Learning Across the Curriculum

Read about how Morse code was developed to send messages via radio or telegraph. Write a sentence in Morse code. Using the code symbols, have your classmates figure out the message.

Broadening Your Understanding

Research how other Native Americans, such as the Choctaws and Comanches, also served as code talkers during World War I and II.

Extending Your Reading

Read one of the following books about Navajo code talkers:

American Indians and World War II, by Alison Bernstein
Navajo Code Talkers, by Nathan Aaseng
Warriors: Navajo Code Talkers, by Kenji Kawano.

Describe the many difficulties the young Navajo recruits had to overcome before they could become code talkers in the Marines.

8 DOCTOR TO ACTOR

When Haing S. Ngor received an Oscar for Best Supporting Actor for *The Killing Fields*, he was stunned. "This is unbelievable," he told the Academy Awards audience. "But so is my entire life."

Ngor began his life in Cambodia. He became a doctor, helping to cure the **afflictions** of poor Cambodian villagers. He earned enough money to live well and to drive expensive cars. However, the Cambodian government was in **turmoil.** After the Khmer Rouge **regime** gained control, its soldiers roamed the cities, killing wealthy and educated people who might oppose Khmer Rouge policies.

After soldiers burst into his operating room, Ngor and his wife fled into the countryside, along with millions of other Cambodians. Despite this **upheaval,** they survived by eating snails, grasshoppers, mice, even leaves—whatever they could find. The journey, however, was too hard for Ngor's wife. Ngor's efforts to save her were to no **avail,** and she soon died.

Eventually, Ngor escaped to Thailand and then to the United States. By chance, producers who were planning the movie *The Killing Fields* saw him at a wedding and asked him to **audition** for the role of Dith Pran, a Cambodian newspaper correspondent. Ngor understood how Pran had suffered under the Khmer Rouge. He expressed his own 34 years of sorrow, **mistrust,** fears, and hopes as he auditioned. His eventual performance in *The Killing Fields* was so convincing that it earned him an Oscar.

Through this movie, Ngor helped the world understand the grief and destruction his homeland had suffered under the **malicious** Khmer Rouge. Although he is now a **celebrity,** Ngor says that most of all he is a survivor of the Cambodian **catastrophe.**

UNDERSTANDING THE STORY

>>>> *Circle the letter next to each correct statement.*

1. The statement that best expresses the main idea of this selection is:
   a. Despite his acting success, Haing Ngor has not forgotten his tragic experiences in Cambodia.
   b. *The Killing Fields* is based on actual events.
   c. The Khmer Rouge brought death and destruction to Cambodia.

2. From this story, you can conclude that
   a. Haing Ngor hopes to set up a medical practice again.
   b. Ngor had hoped to become an actor when he fled to the United States.
   c. Ngor was surprised at his selection for the Oscar.

MAKE AN ALPHABETICAL LIST

>>>> *Here are the ten vocabulary words in this lesson. Write them in alphabetical order in the spaces below.*

regime	avail	catastrophe	celebrity	turmoil
malicious	audition	afflictions	upheaval	mistrust

1. _____   6. _____

2. _____   7. _____

3. _____   8. _____

4. _____   9. _____

5. _____   10. _____

WHAT DO THE WORDS MEAN?

>>>> *Following are some meanings, or definitions, for the ten vocabulary words in this lesson. Write the words next to their definitions.*

1. _____ a famous person

2. _____ seeking to cause harm

3. _____ disaster; tragedy

4. _____ confusion

5. _____ of use or advantage

6. _____ to try out for something

7. _____ disorder

8. _____ pain or suffering

9. _____ the government in power; a form of government

10. _____ a lack of confidence; uncertainty

FIND THE ANALOGIES

>>>> In an **analogy,** the relationship between one pair of words is the same as the relationship between another pair of words. For example, here is one kind of analogy: *sunlight* is to *growth* as *ice* is to *chill*. In this relationship, the first word in each pair causes the effect described by the second word in each pair.

>>>> *See if you can complete the following analogies. Circle the correct word.*

1. **Speed** is to **accidents** as **lie** is to

   a. ticket   b. mistrust   c. truth   d. malicious

2. **Bacteria** is to **infection** as **earthquake** is to

   a. upheaval   b. audition   c. medicine   d. germs

3. **Ice** is to **slipping** as **war** is to

   a. infantry   b. soldiers   c. malicious   d. catastrophe

4. **A job** is to **responsibility** as **regime** is to

   a. president   b. celebrity   c. policies   d. avail

USE YOUR OWN WORDS

>>>> *Look at the picture. What words come into your mind other than the ten vocabulary words used in this lesson? Write them on the lines below. To help you get started, here are two good words:*

1. _____troubled_____

2. _____angry_____

3. _____

4. _____

5. _____

6. _____

7. _____

8. _____

9. _____

10. _____

>>>> An **adverb** is a word that modifies or describes a verb. Adverbs often tell *how*, *when*, or *where*. The adverbs are underlined in the following examples: He walked <u>quickly</u> (how). We are leaving <u>tomorrow</u> (when). Put it <u>down</u> (where).

>>>> *Underline all of the adverbs in the sentences below.*

1. The Cambodian people suffered greatly under the Khmer Rouge.

2. Haing Ngor eventually escaped from Cambodia and slowly made his way to Thailand.

3. Ngor was quietly attending a wedding when his life changed unexpectedly.

4. Today, Ngor is still angry about the way the Khmer Rouge treated his people.

5. Suddenly becoming a celebrity has not drastically changed Ngor's outlook on life.

COMPLETE THE STORY

>>>> Here are the ten vocabulary words for this lesson:

malicious	afflictions	catastrophe	turmoil	upheaval
regime	audition	avail	celebrity	mistrust

>>>> *There are seven blank spaces in the story below. Three vocabulary words have already been used in the story. They are underlined. Use the other seven words to fill in the blanks.*

When Haing S. Ngor went to _____ for the role of Dith Pran in *The Killing Fields,* he took all the <u>turmoil</u> and hurt he had suffered under the Khmer Rouge _____. It was easy for him to portray the _____ Pran had of the Khmer Rouge. Ngor wanted to <u>avail</u> himself of this opportunity to show the _____ caused by the _____ Khmer Rouge.

Now that Ngor is a well-known actor and _____, he has not forgotten the <u>catastrophe</u> that occurred in his homeland. He knows that many people in his native land still suffer the _____ of war.

Learn More About Cambodians

>>>> *On a separate piece of paper or in your notebook or journal, complete one or more of the activities below.*

Building Language

Haing S. Ngor can speak nine languages, including English. List ten advantages of knowing how to speak at least two languages.

Learning Across the Curriculum

Research the history of Cambodia at your library. Then make a timeline showing the changes in Cambodian government from the time the French took over in 1863 until now. Explain how these changes affected the average Cambodian family.

Extending Your Reading

Read the book below about Vithy, a 10-year-old Cambodian boy who escapes from a Khmer Rouge prison camp. Then write a paragraph describing what you learned about the Cambodian people and the physical and emotional destruction of war.

Little Brother, by Allan Baillie

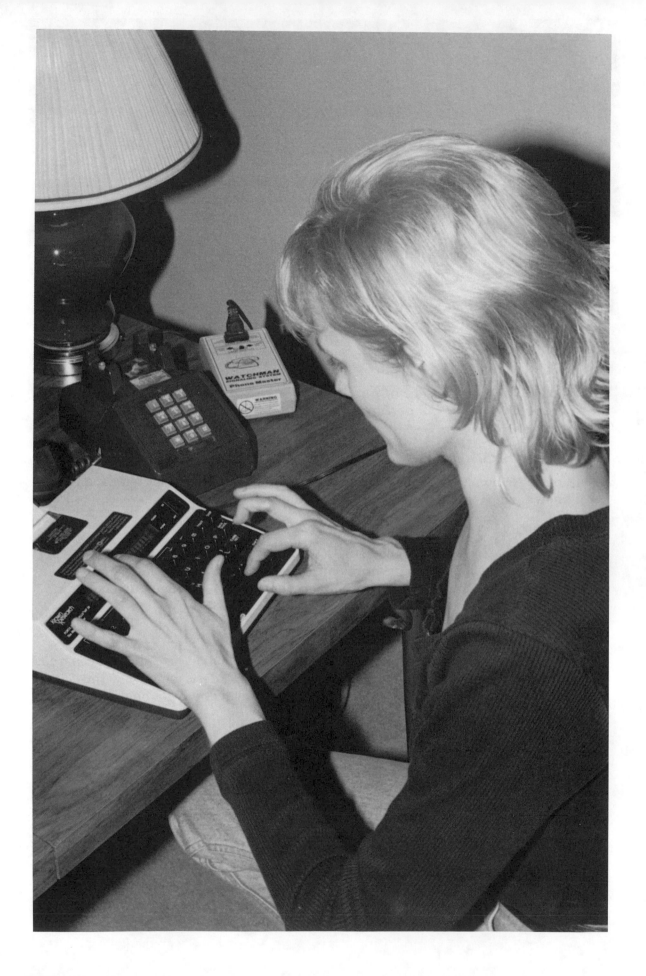

How do people with a hearing loss communicate over the telephone? If speech is not audible to them, they might use a text telephone/telecommunications device for the deaf (TT/TDD) to call a friend who also has a TT/TDD. A TT/TDD combines a phone and a typewriter. Instead of talking, the callers type messages to each other. The messages appear instantaneously on small screens attached to each person's TT/TDD.

A new 24-hour relay service enables hearing-impaired callers to communicate with people who do not have a TT/TDD. The calls require coordination. The caller first dials an 800 number to reach a communications assistant (CA) and then types in a message. The CA calls the hearing person and reads aloud the message. As the hearing person replies orally, the CA types the message for the hearing-impaired caller to read on his or her TT/TDD screen.

Even without a TT/TDD, people with hearing impairments can capitalize on computer networks. Both hearing and hearing-impaired people can communicate through these networks because the entire transaction is displayed on their computer screens.

Two new devices may soon help hearing-impaired people enjoy movies shown at the cinema by converting the actors' dialogue into printed captions. One device is a special pair of glasses that allows viewers to see captions as they watch the screen. A second device is a clear panel that attaches to the arm of the seat. As the viewer watches the movie, captions glow in luminous letters on the panel. Engineers testing these mechanisms are optimistic that they will make movies more fun for hearing-impaired viewers.

UNDERSTANDING THE STORY

>>>> *Circle the letter next to each correct statement.*

1. The statement that best expresses the main idea of this selection is:
   a. New technology has eliminated problems caused by hearing loss.
   b. New technology is helping hearing-impaired people communicate more easily.
   c. Hearing-impaired people should buy a TT/TDD so they can communicate less easily.

2. From this story, you can conclude that
   a. the glasses are the most expensive of the two devices described.
   b. hearing aids do not help people hear over the phone.
   c. additional devices to aid in communications are being researched.

MAKE AN ALPHABETICAL LIST

>>>> *Here are the ten vocabulary words in this lesson. Write them in alphabetical order in the spaces below.*

optimistic	cinema	audible	capitalize	transaction
luminous	captions	instantaneously	mechanism	coordination

1. _____

2. _____

3. _____

4. _____

5. _____

6. _____

7. _____

8. _____

9. _____

10. _____

WHAT DO THE WORDS MEAN?

>>>> *Following are some meanings, or definitions, for the ten vocabulary words in this lesson. Write the words next to their definitions.*

1. _____ expecting excellent results

2. _____ glowing

3. _____ communication or business carried out between two parties

4. _____ motion-picture theater

5. _____ without any delay

6. _____ printed explanations of pictures; dialogue printed on the screen during a movie or television show

7. _____ a process or technique that achieves a certain result

8. _____ to make the most of something

9. _____ capable of being heard

10. _____ the act of helping a complex process work smoothly

FIND THE ANALOGIES

>>>> In an **analogy,** the relationship between one pair of words is the same as the relationship between another pair of words. For example, here is one kind of analogy: *doctor* is to *health* as *florist* is to *bouquet*. In this relationship, the first word in each pair is a worker. The second word in each pair is the worker's product.

>>>> *See if you can complete the following analogies. Circle the correct word.*

1. **Teacher** is to **explanation** as **engineer** is to

   a. luminous   b. mechanism   c. audible   d. captions

2. **Student** is to **learning** as **manager** is to

   a. coordination   b. office   c. study   d. optimistic

3. **Lawyer** is to **acquittal** as **banker** is to

   a. prosecution   b. defendant   c. transaction   d. audible

4. **Architect** is to **buildings** as **police officer** is to

   a. drawings   b. safety   c. police car   d. badge

USE YOUR OWN WORDS

>>>> *Look at the picture. What words come into your mind other than the ten vocabulary words used in this lesson? Write them on the lines below. To help you get started, here are two good words:*

1.   telephone
2.   technical
3. _____
4. _____
5. _____
6. _____
7. _____
8. _____
9. _____
10. _____

IDENTIFY PARTS OF SPEECH

>>>> *The ten vocabulary words in the story represent four different parts of speech. Three of the words are adjectives, one is an adverb, one is a verb, and five are nouns. Write each vocabulary word next to the part of speech that describes its functions.*

Adjectives   _____   _____   _____

Adverb   _____

Verb   _____

Nouns   _____   _____   _____

         _____   _____

COMPLETE THE STORY

>>>> Here are the ten vocabulary words for this lesson:

optimistic	coordination	audible	luminous	transaction
cinema	capitalize	instantaneously	captions	mechanism

>>>> *There are seven blank spaces in the story below. Three vocabulary words have already been used in the story. They are underlined. Use the other seven words to fill in the blanks.*

One _____ being tested for use at the <u>cinema</u> is a panel attached to the arm of the seat that displays <u>captions</u> in _____ letters. When the sound is not _____, the viewer can watch the movie and read the captions _____ .

Some hearing-impaired viewers are eager to _____ on this idea, but the glowing letters tend to distract others at the cinema. An acceptable device requires _____ of the needs of both hearing-impaired and hearing viewers. Cinema owners also have a say in the <u>transaction</u>. Engineers are _____ that they will find a solution to this problem.

Learn More About Hearing Loss

>>>> *On a separate piece of paper or in your notebook or journal, complete one or more of the activities below.*

Learning Across the Curriculum

Find out at what age your school district tests the hearing ability of students. Ask about the test and what it measures. What services does the school district have for students who are hearing impaired? Share the information with your class.

Working Together

The Americans with Disabilities Act (ADA) became law in 1990 and affects about 43 million people. Work with a small group to find out what the ADA requires in one of these categories: access to public accommodations, employment, transportation, state and local government services, or telecommunications. Share your findings with the other groups.

Broadening Your Understanding

Find out how (and whether) people with a hearing loss can access certain services in your community. For example, how would a hearing-impaired person in your community call the emergency squad, phone in a catalog order, or order a meal at a fast-food drive-through?

David Blackwell is a brillant scholar who $\boxed{registered}$ for college at the age of 16. His goal was to earn a bachelor's degree and to go on to teach $\boxed{elementary}$ school. Only six years later, however, he had a Ph.D. in mathematics. He went on to become a professor of $\boxed{statistics}$ at the University of California at Berkeley, where he was well-known for his mathematical $\boxed{theories.}$

Professor Blackwell's success is a $\boxed{testament}$ to his natural ability and to his father's $\boxed{encouragement.}$ Blackwell's father always believed in him and borrowed money to send him to college. When Blackwell found out, he took odd jobs to support himself rather than accept more money from his father. He raised his $\boxed{expectations}$ and changed his goal from being an elementary school teacher to being a college teacher.

After getting his degree, Blackwell taught at Howard University for ten years. At that time, before World War II, it was difficult for African American professors to get jobs at many of the nation's universities. $\boxed{Views}$ changed, however, and by 1954, Blackwell was teaching statistical mathematics at Berkeley in California. Later, he became chairman of the mathematics department. He retired in 1989.

One might say that Professor Blackwell could not $\boxed{resist}$ doing what came so naturally to him—teaching. When asked why he chose to teach, he replied, "Why do you want to share something beautiful with somebody else? Because in $\boxed{transmitting}$ it, you appreciate its beauty all over again."

UNDERSTANDING THE STORY

>>>> *Circle the letter next to each correct statement.*

1. The statement that best expresses the main idea of this selection is:
    a. David Blackwell has never enjoyed research.
    b. David Blackwell always sets high standards for himself.
    c. Professor Blackwell is a natural-born teacher.

2. David Blackwell worked at a variety of odd jobs during his college career because
    a. he didn't want to take any more money from his father.
    b. he had lost his scholarship.
    c. his parents couldn't support him.

MAKE AN ALPHABETICAL LIST

>>>> *Here are the ten vocabulary words in this lesson. Write them in alphabetical order in the spaces below.*

registered	encouragement	elementary	expectations	statistics
views	theories	resist	testament	transmitting

1. _____
2. _____
3. _____
4. _____
5. _____

6. _____
7. _____
8. _____
9. _____
10. _____

WHAT DO THE WORDS MEAN?

>>>> *Following are some meanings, or definitions, for the ten vocabulary words in this lesson. Write the words next to their definitions.*

1. _____ support

2. _____ hopes; prospects

3. _____ ideas about how something might be

4. _____ fundamental or simplest part

5. _____ clear evidence, proof

6. _____ withstand

7. _____ field of mathematics

8. _____ officially enrolled

9. _____ attitude; opinions

10. _____ sending or transferring from one person or place to another

FIND THE ANALOGIES

>>>> In an **analogy**, similar relationships occur between words that are different. For example, *pig* is to *hog* as *car* is to *automobile*. The relationship is that the words mean the same. Here's another analogy: *noisy* is to *quiet* as *short* is to *tall*. In this relationship, the words have opposite meanings.

>>>> *See if you can complete the following analogies. Circle the correct word.*

1. **Elementary** is to **advanced** as **cherishing** is to

   a. loving   b. thinking   c. disliking   d. exaggerating

2. **Views** are to **beliefs** as **concerned** is to

   a. indifferent   b. justified   c. worried   d. satisfied

3. **Theories** are to **facts** as **forceful** is to

   a. weak   b. peaceful   c. vigorous   d. delightful

4. **Encouragment** is to **guidance** as **elevate** is to

   a. change   b. raise   c. lower   d. throw

USE YOUR OWN WORDS

>>>> *Look at the picture. What words come into your mind other than the ten vocabulary words used in this lesson? Write them on the lines below. To help you get started, here are two good words:*

1. _____kind_____
2. _____scholarly_____
3. _____
4. _____
5. _____
6. _____
7. _____
8. _____
9. _____
10. _____

FIND SOME SYNONYMS

>>>> The story you read has many interesting words that were not listed as vocabulary words. Six of these words are *brilliant*, *scholar*, *appreciate*, *support*, *research*, and *universities*.

>>>> *Can you think of a synonym for each of these words? Remember: a synonym is a word that means the same as another word. Sorrowful and sad are synonyms. Write a synonym in the space next to each word.*

1. brilliant _____   4. scholar _____

2. appreciate _____   5. support _____

3. well-known _____   6. universities _____

COMPLETE THE STORY

>>>> Here are the ten vocabulary words for this lesson:

views	theories	registered	statistics	elementary
encouragement	expectations	testament	resist	transmitting

>>>> *There are seven blank spaces in the story below. Three vocabulary words have already been used in the story. They are underlined. Use the other seven words to fill in the blanks.*

Professor Blackwell has contributed many important _____ to the field of statistics. In addition to these contributions, he was a well-respected administrator and teacher. Students _____ for his courses in large numbers over the years. He succeeded in _____ his wealth of knowledge to many of these students. His views toward his students were always positive. Their high opinions of him were a _____ to the success of his methods. Throughout his career, the _____ of others in his field helped when he was looking for work. He repaid their kindness by setting high expectations for his own students, who always tried hard to meet those high goals. Professor Blackwell was an inspired professor. He could never _____ the challenge of learning—and then teaching—all there is to know in the field of statistics. It is likely that his students will continue his tradition of setting high standards in _____ schools and high schools throughout the country.

Learn More About Inspiring People

>>>> *On a separate piece of paper or in your notebook or journal, complete one or more of the activities below.*

Learning Across the Curriculum

What subject do you find easy to learn about? Why? Explain how this information can help you learn about other things better.

Broadening Your Understanding

Think about your favorite teacher in school. First, complete a list of questions to ask the teacher about how he or she tries to inspire students. Next, interview the teacher. Finally, write what you learn in the form of a newspaper feature article.

Extending Your Reading

Jaime Escalante is another teacher who loves to teach. Escalante teaches math in a high school in East L.A. His success led to national recognition and to a movie about his work named *Stand and Deliver*. Read the following book about Jaime Escalante. Then write why you think Escalante is such a successful teacher.

Escalante: The Best Teacher in America, by Jay Mathews

Itzhak Perlman was born in Tel Aviv, Israel, the only child of Polish **emigrants.** As early as the age of 2, he sang along with the operas that were broadcast over the radio. He loved music and from an early age wanted to be a musician.

When he was 4 years old, he got **polio.** His parents feared that his illness would make him a **melancholy** child, so they bought him a violin to cheer him up. He practiced the violin daily without becoming **perturbed.** "Polio didn't stop me," he proclaimed. "I played the violin and even played soccer in the streets. With my leg braces and crutches, I blocked anything!"

Perlman came to the United States to represent Israel in a violin competition. He was such an incredible success that his family decided to remain in the United States. His fame as a concert violinist soared.

The violin is one of the hardest instruments to play. Every solo violinist stands so that the weight of his or her body is behind the bow. Perlman's **disability** prevents him from standing. Even though he remains seated while playing, his tones are beautiful. Other violinists have praised Perlman for his perfect pitch and great **accuracy.**

His success as one of the greatest violinists in the world has brought **prosperity** to him and his family. With his earnings, he gives money to a **lobby** group to help pass laws to aid people with disabilities. He knows firsthand that better services and **facilities** are needed. Itzhak Perlman's talent seems **limitless** and his courage boundless.

UNDERSTANDING THE STORY

>>>> *Circle the letter next to each correct statement.*

1. The statement that best expresses the main idea of this selection is:
   a. Itzhak Perlman overcame a disability to achieve fame as a great violinist.
   b. Itzhak Perlman has always enjoyed music.
   c. Itzhak Perlman is involved in writing laws to aid people with disabilities.

2. From this story, you can conclude that
   a. Itzhak Perlman's family is happy about his tremendous success.
   b. Itzhak Perlman's courage will help him overcome other hardships in life.
   c. Itzhak Perlman's son will become a great violinist.

MAKE AN ALPHABETICAL LIST

>>>> *Here are the ten vocabulary words in this lesson. Write them in alphabetical order in the spaces below.*

perturbed	disability	melancholy	limitless	emigrants
accuracy	lobby	polio	prosperity	facilities

1. _____

2. _____

3. _____

4. _____

5. _____

6. _____

7. _____

8. _____

9. _____

10. _____

WHAT DO THE WORDS MEAN?

>>>> *Following are some meanings, or definitions, for the ten vocabulary words in this lesson. Write the words next to their definitions.*

1. _____ upset; troubled

2. _____ a crippling disease that paralyzes certain muscles

3. _____ sad; gloomy

4. _____ correctness; skillfulness

5. _____ well being or wealth, usually financial

6. _____ people who leave one country to settle in another

7. _____ never ending; without limit

8. _____ equipment to help people do things more easily

9. _____ a disadvantage that makes activities very difficult

10. _____ a pressure group; a special-interest group to influence lawmakers

FIND THE ANALOGIES

>>>> In an **analogy,** similar relationships occur between words that are different. For example, *pig* is to *hog* as *car* is to *automobile*. The relationship is that the words mean the same. Here's another analogy: *noisy* is to *quiet* as *short* is to *tall*. In this relationship, the words have opposite meanings.

>>>> *See if you can complete the following analogies. Circle the correct word.*

1. **Limitless** is to **end** as **polio** is to

   a. health   b. politics   c. disease   d. polo

2. **Melancholy** is to **happiness** as **difficulty** is to

   a. impossibility   b. ease   c. effort   d. laziness

3. **Perturbed** is to **disturbed** as **understood** is to

   a. burdened   b. misunderstood   c. comprehended   d. upset

4. **Prosperity** is to **wealth** as **emigrant** is to

   a. tourist   b. foreigner   c. newcomer   d. friend

5. **Accuracy** is to **truth** as **error** is to

   a. misfortune   b. dislike   c. mistake   d. errand

USE YOUR OWN WORDS

>>>> *Look at the picture. What words come into your mind other than the ten vocabulary words used in this lesson? Write them on the lines below. To help you get started, here are two good words:*

1. _____ smile _____
2. _____ bow tie _____
3. _____
4. _____
5. _____
6. _____
7. _____
8. _____
9. _____
10. _____

MAKE POSSESSIVE WORDS

>>>> The singular possessive of a word shows that something belongs to it. For example, Bill has a boat, so it is *Bill's* boat. To make a possessive of a word that is singular, add an apostrophe and an *s* to the word, such as *baker's* bread or *class's* teacher. To make a possessive of a plural word that ends in *s*, add an apostrophe only, such as *friends'* bicycles or *ladies'* hats. To make a possessive of a plural word that does not end in *s*, add an apostrophe and an *s*, such as *children's* toys.

>>>> *Here are ten words from the story. In the space next to each word, write the correct possessive of the word.*

1. musician _____
2. Perlman _____
3. bow _____
4. instrument _____
5. concert _____

6. musicians _____
7. child _____
8. violin _____
9. boy _____
10. family _____

COMPLETE THE STORY

>>>> Here are the ten vocabulary words for this lesson:

disability	emigrants	prosperity	perturbed	accuracy
limitless	lobby	polio	facilities	melancholy

>>>> *There are seven blank spaces in the story below. Three vocabulary words have already been used in the story. They are underlined. Use the other seven words to fill in the blanks.*

At the age of 4, Itzhak Perlman was stricken with a disease called _____. He played ball and refused to be _____ by his illness. In spite of his <u>disability,</u> he practiced the violin daily. He plays with great skill and _____. His talent seems <u>limitless.</u>

Perlman and his family are _____ of Israel. Shortly after they came to this country, Perlman became ill. His parents feared that he would become <u>melancholy.</u>

Perlman's success has brought him fame and _____. He works for people with disabilities and hopes to get better _____ for them. He contributes money to a _____ group that can influence the lawmakers in favor of people with disabilities.

Learn More About Music

>>>> *On a separate piece of paper or in your notebook or journal, complete one or more of the activities below.*

Appreciating Diversity

Think about a kind of music that is popular in your native language. Listen to it and find out more about its history. Give a report to your class and include some of the music to illustrate your points.

Learning Across the Curriculum

Some therapists help troubled people by using music. Find out more about how music therapy works and write about it. Do you think this kind of therapy would be successful?

Broadening Your Understanding

Listen to a recording by Itzhak Perlman. As you listen, think about why he is so respected by other musicians and why he is so popular with the public. What makes his work exceptional? Write what you think after you finish listening to him play.

Mother Teresa is a tiny woman of Slavic descent. But she has achieved greatness in caring for the destitute in India. She has been described as someone "through whom the light of God shines."

As a girl, Agnes Gonxha Bojaxhiu dreamed of becoming a nun. After taking her vows, she worked as an English teacher. Later, she became the principal of Saint Mary's High School in Calcutta. This was an exclusive Catholic school for girls.

After 17 years, she left Saint Mary's. She felt she had a calling to live and work among the poor. Bojaxhiu had no money and no place to live. Somehow, she knew God would take care of her. She took the name of Saint Teresa, who advocated doing good by helping the poor.

Mother Teresa began her work by setting up a home where sick people could be cared for. Soon others joined her in her efforts. Her organization now cares for many different groups of people. Homes for abandoned children and workshops for the unemployed or incapacitated are just a few of Mother Teresa's programs. The only entrance requirements are that a person be poor and in need of help. Others have set up similar programs around the world. For example, they have organized free-lunch programs for the poor and the desolate.

The money to support Mother Teresa's programs pours in from all parts of the world. The news of her good works for the oppressed has spread. In 1979, Mother Teresa received the Nobel Peace Prize. The prize honored her and the thousands of people she has helped.

UNDERSTANDING THE STORY

>>>> *Circle the letter next to each correct statement.*

1. The statement that best expresses the main idea of this selection is:
   a. India needs Mother Teresa's help more than other countries.
   b. Mother Teresa's unselfish devotion to others has improved life for many poor people.
   c. Mother Teresa is always looking for people to continue her work.

2. From this story, you can conclude that
   a. Mother Teresa will join the United Nations to improve life everywhere.
   b. Mother Teresa's work will bring an end to poverty everywhere.
   c. Mother Teresa will continue her good works on behalf of all oppressed people.

MAKE AN ALPHABETICAL LIST

>>>> *Here are the ten vocabulary words in this lesson. Write them in alphabetical order in the spaces below.*

destitute	exclusive	incapacitated	descent	oppressed
advocated	similar	requirements	organization	desolate

1. _____   6. _____

2. _____   7. _____

3. _____   8. _____

4. _____   9. _____

5. _____   10. _____

WHAT DO THE WORDS MEAN?

>>>> *Following are some meanings, or definitions, for the ten vocabulary words in this lesson. Write the words next to their definitions.*

1. _____ the same; alike

2. _____ poor; needy; deprived

3. _____ persecuted; crushed; overburdened

4. _____ lonely; abandoned; miserable

5. _____ one and only; open only to the upper classes or the wealthy

6. _____ things wanted or needed; demands

7. _____ unable to function in some way

8. _____ system; structure; plan

9. _____ favored; recommended

10. _____ ancestry; origin

FIND THE ANALOGIES

>>>> In an **analogy,** similar relationships occur between words that are different. For example, *pig* is to *hog* as *car* is to *automobile*. The relationship is that the words mean the same. Here's another analogy: *noisy* is to *quiet* as *short* is to *tall*. In this relationship, the words have opposite meanings.

>>>> *See if you can complete the following analogies. Circle the correct word.*

1. **Destitute** is to **desolate** as **miserable** is to

    a. downtrodden   b. joyous   c. important   d. uncertain

2. **Oppressed** is to **dominated** as **excluded** is to

    a. barred   b. invited   c. fulfilled   d. separated

3. **Advocated** is to **fought** for as **delighted** is to

    a. needed   b. pleased   c. depressed   d. finished

4. **Similar** is to **same** as **definite** is to

    a. indefinite   b. bold   c. specific   d. detailed

5. **Requirements** is to **demands** as **essentials** is to

    a. entries   b. necessities   c. actions   d. requests

USE YOUR OWN WORDS

>>>> *Look at the picture. What words come into your mind other than the ten vocabulary words used in this lesson? Write them on the lines below. To help you get started, here are two good words:*

1.   sincere
2.   habit
3. _____
4. _____
5. _____
6. _____
7. _____
8. _____
9. _____
10. _____

DO THE CROSSWORD PUZZLE

>>>> *The following crossword puzzle uses vocabulary words from this lesson. Look at the first definition under the "Across" column. Which vocabulary word does it define?* Oppressed *is the correct answer. Now, write one letter from* oppressed *in each of the nine empty boxes in the "1-Across" row. Complete the rest of the puzzle in the same manner.*

Across

1. crushed

4. unique

5. abandoned

6. unable to function

Down

2. demands

3. alike

COMPLETE THE STORY

>>>> Here are the ten vocabulary words for this lesson:

incapacitated	oppressed	desolate	exclusive	requirements
descent	similar	organization	advocated	destitute

>>>> *There are seven blank spaces in the story below. Three vocabulary words have already been used in the story. They are underlined. Use the other seven words to fill in the blanks.*

Agnes Gonxha Bojaxhiu is of Slavic _____. She chose to become a nun to help the <u>oppressed</u>. She became a teacher in India at an _____ school for girls. She felt called to serve the _____ among India's poor. No human being is too <u>desolate</u> for help. She created an _____ to help children who are homeless.

Influential people in India help her. With their money, she sets up schools without _____ that educate and train the poor. She and her volunteers set up <u>similar</u> programs all over the world. Her workshops help those who are _____ get jobs and care for themselves. Her beliefs have always _____ helping others by doing the humblest of jobs.

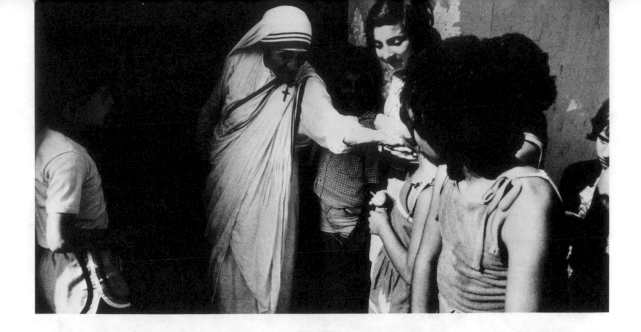

Learn More About Helping Others

>>>> *On a separate piece of paper or in your notebook or journal, complete one or more of the activities below.*

Working Together

There are many ways a group of people can make an impact on the world around them. In your group, brainstorm what you could do for others in your community. Then have different students research possibilities. When you have gathered all the information, make a plan to help your community and carry it out. Report to your class about what you have done.

Learning Across the Curriculum

Find out who won the most recent Nobel Peace Prize. Research the background of the person or persons who won and the history of the dispute or problem that led to the award. Report to the class on your findings.

Broadening Your Understanding

In every community, there are groups that help others. Find out who is helping your community and write a report about the group that most interests you. Who started the group? Why? What difference is the group making in your community? How can high school students get involved? Share your report with the class.

13 OUT OF THE GARDEN

After three days of riots that *disrupted* their lives, students at Crenshaw High School in south-central Los Angeles stood in the middle of the ashes and *contemplated* the ruins around them. Their final *analysis* was that if their lives were ever going to get better, it was up to them.

They began by planting a garden behind the school and calling their enterprise "Food from the 'Hood." They planned to sell the vegetables, donate some of their profits to the needy, and put the rest of the money into college scholarships. They felt *dejected* when they *computed* their first-year's profits—only $600.

Because of all that lettuce in their garden, they decided to make salad dressing. After receiving grants from the city's riot-recovery agency, the young people developed their first batch of creamy Italian dressing, using basil and parsley they grew themselves. For six months they experimented with recipes, making the use of all-natural ingredients a *priority*. By April 1994, they had a low-fat product that impressed everyone with its quality and flavor. With the advice of marketing executive Melinda McMullen, the group created their own packaging and developed a marketing plan for their *commodity*.

Now their product, Straight Out 'the Garden, is sold at 2,000 grocery stores in 23 states. In June 1994, three of their members shared $7,000 in scholarships. The group hopes its scholarship fund will *surpass* $100,000 by June 1995. The students are already considering repairing an old greenhouse so that basil and parsley can be grown year-round.

"Food from the 'Hood" has left an *indelible* impression on south-central Los Angeles by demonstrating that hard work and hope still work despite *overwhelming* odds.

UNDERSTANDING THE STORY

>>>> *Circle the letter next to each correct statement.*

1. The statement that best expresses the main idea of this selection is:
   a. Selling vegetables from a garden does not raise much money.
   b. Young people do not need the advice of adults in order to be successful.
   c. A group of young people has found a way to learn important skills and raise money for college.

2. From this story, you can conclude that
   a. other young people might also be successful in introducing a new product.
   b. young people in other cities should try selling salad dressing.
   c. "Food from the 'Hood" would not be successful anywhere but in Los Angeles.

75

MAKE AN ALPHABETICAL LIST

>>>> *Here are the ten vocabulary words in this lesson. Write them in alphabetical order in the spaces below.*

computed	disrupted	surpass	commodity	overwhelming
dejected	priority	analysis	indelible	contemplated

1. _____

2. _____

3. _____

4. _____

5. _____

6. _____

7. _____

8. _____

9. _____

10. _____

WHAT DO THE WORDS MEAN?

>>>> *Following are some meanings, or definitions, for the ten vocabulary words in this lesson. Write the words next to their definitions.*

1. _____ something that cannot be removed or erased

2. _____ threw into disorder

3. _____ considered; thought about

4. _____ a product; something useful

5. _____ breaking something complex into parts and examining the parts

6. _____ depressed

7. _____ to exceed or go beyond

8. _____ figured out; calculated

9. _____ a position of importance; something that comes first

10. _____ overpowering

FIND THE ANALOGIES

>>>> In an **analogy,** the relationship between one pair of words is the same as the relationship between another pair or words. For example, here is one kind of analogy: *sunlight* is to *growth* as *ice* is to *chill*. In this relationship, the first word in each pair causes the effect described by the second word in each pair.

>>>> *See if you can complete the following analogies. Circle the correct word.*

1. **Compliment** is to **pleased** as **failure** is to

   a. flattered   b. satisfied   c. dejected   d. disrupted

2. **Refuse** is to **anger** as **surpass** is to

   a. impress   b. fail   c. anguish   d. contemplate

3. **Routine** is to **boredom** as **imagination** is to

   a. disrupted   b. overwhelming   c. ideas   d. priority

4. **Advertising** is to **sales** as **manufacturing** is to

   a. commercial   b. commodity   c. computed   d. profit

USE YOUR OWN WORDS

>>>> *Look at the picture. What words come into your mind other than the ten vocabulary words used in this lesson? Write them on the lines below. To help you get started, here are two good words:*

1. _____profit_____
2. _____groceries_____
3. _____
4. _____
5. _____
6. _____
7. _____
8. _____
9. _____
10. _____

77

USE ANOTHER FORM OF THE WORD

>>>> One word can have several different forms. For example, *act* is a verb, *action* is a noun, *active* is an adjective, and *actively* is an adverb. The correct form of the word depends on its use in the sentence.

>>>> *Complete each sentence below by writing in the correct form of the word at the end of the sentence.*

1. The odds facing the young people were _____. (overwhelm)

2. The 1992 riots were a _____ in their lives. (disrupt)

3. At the end of their first year of gardening, they _____ their profits. (computer)

4. The group had no _____ experience in business. (priority)

5. They were dejected by the first year's profits, but they were _____ to continue. (determination)

COMPLETE THE STORY

>>>> Here are the ten vocabulary words for this lesson:

dejected	overwhelming	surpass	analysis	disrupted
commodity	indelible	priority	computed	contemplated

>>>> *There are seven blanks in the story below. Three vocabulary words have already been used in the story. They are underlined. Use the other seven words to fill in the blanks.*

The _____ success of "Food from the 'Hood" has made an <u>indelible</u> impression on many people. It's a good thing that no one _____ the group's chances of succeeding before the young people started their garden. The _____ would have shown no marketable <u>commodity</u> in a community totally _____ by the 1992 riots. After group members _____ their chances of success, they might have become _____ and given up. Instead, they made research a <u>priority</u>. By carefully analyzing the market for salad dressing, they have been able to _____ their own wildest dreams.

Learn More About Consumerism

>>>> *On a separate piece of paper or in your notebook or journal, complete one or more of the activities below.*

Learning Across the Curriculum

Straight out 'the Garden salad dressing costs $2.59 a bottle. If "Food from the 'Hood" makes a 10 percent profit on each bottle, how much does it cost to produce and market each bottle?

Working Together

Work with a small group to identify a product that young people could make and sell at a profit in your school or community. Share your commodity idea with the other groups. (Consider researching what it would require to produce the product.)

Broadening Your Understanding

Working as a group, find out how other locally produced products are marketed in your community. Then make a plan for marketing a product that your group might produce. Include plans for distributing the product to consumers. Make a calendar to show the timing of different parts of your operation.

14 PLAYING IT TOUGH

Actress Sigourney Weaver is making a movie career of *portraying* strong women. In *Alien, Aliens,* and *Alien 3,* she fights monsters. In *Ghostbusters,* she tangles with a *demon.* She mothers a group of 450-pound apes in *Gorillas in the Mist.* In *Working Girl,* she is a businesswoman who is *determined* to get what she wants. In *Dave,* she plays an imposing First Lady.

Who is this talented, *innovative* actress? Weaver was born Susan Weaver. She changed her name to Sigourney when she was 14 years old. "I was so tall [5' 10½"]," she explains, "and Susan is such a short name." She *considers* Sigourney to be a better stage name —"long and curvy, with a musical ring."

Although her parents were both in show business, Weaver became an actress without her family's help. She *enrolled* in drama school at Stanford and then Yale. Later she performed on the Broadway stage and in daytime TV shows. When Weaver landed the part of Ripley in *Alien,* her career really *soared.*

Now that Weaver is an *acknowledged* movie star, she plans to continue playing *dynamic* characters. It disturbs her to see women in weak roles. According to Weaver, in the movies, men *dominate* the action. She asks, "Doesn't anyone know that women are incredibly strong?"

UNDERSTANDING THE STORY

>>>> *Circle the letter next to each correct statement.*

1. The statement that best expresses the main idea of this selection is:
   a. Sigourney Weaver became a successful actress entirely on her own.
   b. Sigourney Weaver changed her name because Sigourney is a better stage name than Susan.
   c. Sigourney Weaver is a talented actress who is known for playing forceful women.

2. From this story, you can conclude that
   a. Sigourney Weaver makes her own decisions.
   b. there are no men in Weaver's movies.
   c. Weaver doesn't get along with her family.

MAKE AN ALPHABETICAL LIST

>>>> *Here are the ten vocabulary words in this lesson. Write them in alphabetical order in the spaces below.*

soared	dynamic	enrolled	innovative	acknowledged
portraying	dominate	demon	determined	considers

1. _____   6. _____

2. _____   7. _____

3. _____   8. _____

4. _____   9. _____

5. _____   10. _____

WHAT DO THE WORDS MEAN?

>>>> *Following are some meanings, or definitions, for the ten vocabulary words in this lesson. Write the words next to their definitions.*

1. _____ having one's own mind made up; strong willed

2. _____ entered; joined; registered

3. _____ control; rule

4. _____ an evil spirit; devil

5. _____ believes; thinks of; regards

6. _____ playing the role of; representing

7. _____ generally recognized or accepted

8. _____ forceful; energetic; active

9. _____ able to do things in a new way; creative

10. _____ moved upward; rose above the ordinary

FIND THE ANALOGIES

>>>> In an **analogy,** similar relationships occur between words that are different. For example, *pig* is to *hog* as *car* is to *automobile*. The relationship is that the words mean the same. Here's another analogy: *noisy* is to *quiet* as *short* is to *tall*. In this relationship, the words have opposite meanings.

>>>> *See if you can complete the following analogies. Circle the correct word.*

1. **Soared** is to **plunged** as **wealthy** is to

    a. rich   b. greedy   c. poor   d. royal

2. **Demon** is to **angel** as **solid** is to

    a. rock   b. devil   c. liquid   d. freezer

3. **Dominate** is to **control** as **gather** is to

    a. rule   b. collect   c. scatter   d. earn

4. **Acknowledged** is to **accepted** as **innovative** is to

    a. creative   b. innocent   c. rejected   d. usual

5. **Determined** is to **uncertain** as **careful** is to

    a. watchful   b. brave   c. unpleasant   d. reckless

USE YOUR OWN WORDS

>>>> *Look at the picture. What words come into your mind other than the ten vocabulary words used in this lesson? Write them on the lines below. To help you get started, here are two good words:*

1. _____ pretty _____

2. _____ earring _____

3. _____

4. _____

5. _____

6. _____

7. _____

8. _____

9. _____

10. _____

DO THE CROSSWORD PUZZLE

>>>> *The following crossword puzzle uses vocabulary words from this lesson. Look at the first definition under the "Across" column. Which vocabulary word does it define? Determined is the correct answer. Now write one letter from determined in each of the ten empty boxes in the "1-Across" row. Complete the rest of the puzzle in the same manner.*

Across

1. strong-willed

4. devil

5. having great energy

Down

2. became a member of

3. creative

4. take control of

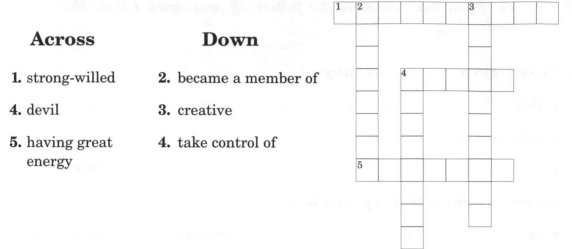

COMPLETE THE STORY

>>>> Here are the ten vocabulary words for this lesson:

considers	dominate	acknowledged	innovative	dynamic
enrolled	portraying	determined	soared	demon

>>>> *There are seven blank spaces in the story below. Three vocabulary words have already been used in the story. They are underlined. Use the other seven words to fill in the blanks.*

   Few actresses can _____ a scene like Sigourney Weaver. She was <u>acknowledged</u> to be a perfect choice for the part of Ripley in *Alien*. With that role, her popularity among moviegoers _____.

   Weaver was <u>determined</u> to succeed on her own. That is why she refused her parents' assistance when she _____ in drama school. She displays the same drive in her movies when she faces a monster or a _____. Obviously, she is a <u>dynamic</u> person both on and off the screen.

   Weaver will continue _____ strong women in _____ roles. She _____ this being faithful to her art and to herself.

84

Learn More About Strong Women

>>>> *On a separate piece of paper or in your notebook or journal, complete one or more of the activities below.*

Learning Across the Curriculum

Although men are generally physically stronger, women have many biological advantages over men. Research what some of these advantages are and write about them.

Broadening Your Understanding

Think about what Sigourney Weaver said about being a strong woman and about the parts that she has played. Consider what you think a strong woman is. Write a one-act play with a part for a strong woman.

Extending Your Reading

Read one of the following books about women in the arts. Then choose someone you read about. Write whether you think the person is strong, and if so, how she shows her strength.

Marion Anderson, by Anne Tedards
Visions: Stories about Women Artists, by Leslie Sills
Women Music Makers, by Janet Nichols
Katherine Dunham, by Jeannine Dominy

Maya Angelou's *pursuit* of different careers has been most unusual. She has been an author, actress, singer, dancer, songwriter, teacher, and editor. Her *creativity* ranks her at the top of each field.

Angelou's autobiography, *I Know Why the Caged Bird Sings*, has been praised for its honesty and power. She mentions that she was only 3 years old when her parents were *divorced.* Angelou triumphed over this *adversity* with the help of her grandmother.

Despite *discrimination,* there have been many *variations* in Angelou's career. She toured Europe and Africa as one of the leads in *Porgy and Bess.* Her restless spirit took her to Africa, where she edited newspapers. At Ghana University, she served as head of the music and drama departments.

Back in America, Angelou wrote songs, poetry, and two plays. She also *participated* in the "Black Heritage" TV series, in which artists from various fields gave *versions* of their own creative development. To Angelou, *continuity* is basic to any creative development. She continued her own development by writing and reading the first inaugural poem in 32 years, at President Clinton's inauguration in 1992.

French, Spanish, Italian, Arabic, and Fanti—a West African tongue—are languages she speaks and writes fluently. Maya Angelou is talented but not *arrogant* and believes that love can build anything.

UNDERSTANDING THE STORY

>>>> *Circle the letter next to each correct statement.*

1. The statement that best expresses the main idea of this selection is:
   a. Maya Angelou doesn't believe in wasting talent by doing too many things.
   b. Angelou's life is proof that if one has talent and courage, nothing is impossible.
   c. Maya Angelou has enjoyed life because she has fought hard for civil rights.

2. From this story, you can conclude that
   a. Maya Angelou will start a scholarship fund for talented young people.
   b. Maya Angelou will write another play.
   c. Maya Angelou will continue to work hard and explore new fields.

MAKE AN ALPHABETICAL LIST

>>>> *Here are the ten vocabulary words in this lesson. Write them in alphabetical order in the spaces below.*

divorced	arrogant	variations	participated	discrimination
adversity	creativity	continuity	pursuit	versions

1. _____ 6. _____

2. _____ 7. _____

3. _____ 8. _____

4. _____ 9. _____

5. _____ 10. _____

WHAT DO THE WORDS MEAN?

>>>> *Following are some meanings, or definitions, for the ten vocabulary words in this lesson. Write the words next to their definitions.*

1. _____ proud; acting superior

2. _____ effort to secure something; search

3. _____ changes; alterations

4. _____ misfortune; bad luck; hardship

5. _____ lasting; progression

6. _____ prejudice; acting unfairly against someone

7. _____ no longer married

8. _____ imagination; originality; artistic talent

9. _____ became actively involved; took part in; cooperated

10. _____ points of view; different ways of looking at things

FIND THE ANALOGIES

>>>> In an **analogy,** similar relationships occur between words that are different. For example, *pig* is to *hog* as *car* is to *automobile.* The relationship is that the words mean the same. Here's another analogy: *noisy* is to *quiet* as *short* is to *tall.* In this relationship, the words have opposite meanings.

>>>> *See if you can complete the following analogies. Circle the correct word.*

1. Adversity is to **hardship** as **prejudice** is to

    a. uncertainty   b. discrimination   c. justice   d. fortune

2. Creativity is to **imitation** as **laughter** is to

    a. pain   b. tears   c. joy   d. hope

3. Participated is to **engaged** as **rushed** is to

    a. hurried   b. stood   c. found   d. decided

4. Divorce is to **marriage** as **courage** is to

    a. cowardice   b. helplessness   c. bravery   d. separation

5. Arrogant is to **modest** as **foreign** is to

    a. important   b. domestic   c. wonderful   d. wholesome

USE YOUR OWN WORDS

>>>> *Look at the picture. What words come into your mind other than the ten vocabulary words used in this lesson? Write them on the lines below. To help you get started, here are two good words:*

1.   bright
2.   thoughtful
3. _____
4. _____
5. _____
6. _____
7. _____
8. _____
9. _____
10. _____

MATCH THE ANTONYMS

>>>> **Antonyms** are words that are opposite in meaning. For example, *good* and *bad* and *heavy* and *light* are antonyms.

>>>> *Match the vocabulary words on the left with the antonyms on the right. Write the correct letter in the space.*

Vocabulary Words

1. _____ divorced
2. _____ continuity
3. _____ arrogant
4. _____ discrimination
5. _____ variations
6. _____ adversity

Antonyms

a. humble
b. fairness
c. married
d. interruption
e. happiness
f. similarities

COMPLETE THE STORY

>>>> Here are the ten vocabulary words for this lesson:

adversity	variations	arrogant	versions	discrimination
pursuit	divorced	participated	creativity	continuity

>>>> *There are seven blank spaces in the story below. Three vocabulary words have already been used in the story. They are underlined. Use the other seven words to fill in the blanks.*

Maya Angelou's life story has been a victory over _____. As a young child, she experienced hardship when her parents were _____. Early in her life, Angelou showed that she could fight <u>discrimination</u> by working for what she believed in. Her careers show many _____; they include being a writer, dancer, poet, and teacher. Her <u>pursuit</u> of different careers is a mark of her many talents and abilities. She has _____ in many different fields of activity, and her contributions are astounding. In one TV series with Bill Moyers, Angelou and other artists related different <u>versions</u> of how they developed creatively. Some people who have achieved such great success are _____, but that is not true of Angelou. She is sweet and modest. She strongly believes that it is important to have _____ if one is to achieve success. The _____ in all her artistic careers has been at an unusually high level.

Learn More About Maya Angelou

>>>> *On a separate piece of paper or in your notebook or journal, complete one or more of the activities below.*

Learning Across the Curriculum

Find out more about Ghana, where Maya Angelou served as head of the music and drama departments of Ghana University. Write a report that tells about the people who live in Ghana, what they do, and how they live. Then explain how Angelou's time in Ghana might have influenced what she writes now.

Broadening Your Understanding

Find a copy of the poem that Maya Angelou read at Bill Clinton's Presidential inauguration. Read it. What do you think the poet is saying? Write what you think the poem means.

Extending Your Reading

Read one of the following novels or collections of poems by Maya Angelou. Write a review of the book that could appear in a newspaper.

I Know Why the Caged Bird Sings
Soul Looks Back in Wonder
Life Doesn't Frighten Me at All
Pocket Poems
Wouldn't Take Nothing for My Journey Now

As a child, Steven Spielberg liked to try out his ideas on his three younger sisters—Susan, Anne, and Nancy. If you have seen *Jaws, Poltergeist, ET, Gremlins, Raiders of the Lost Ark, Indiana Jones and the Temple of Doom, Jurassic Park,* or any other Spielberg movie, you can imagine that the girls had a scary childhood.

Spielberg once told his sisters that a World War II pilot had died in their closet and rotted there. They did not believe him—until they opened the door and saw a *repulsive* skull in a pilot's cap and aviator goggles, planted there by their loving brother.

Spielberg himself had a lonely childhood. His family moved frequently, so he was often the new kid at school. Bullies liked to *antagonize* this skinny boy who was not good at sports or academics. Spielberg was good at filming movies, though, and had already chosen his lifelong career by the time he was 12 years old.

After his family moved to California, Spielberg started college and made several films. People at Universal Studios saw the films, recognized their high *caliber,* and asked the 21-year-old Spielberg to direct some television series. Eventually, Spielberg's job *evolved* into directing movies. Throughout his career, Spielberg has used technology to create ferocious and *endearing* creatures from the deep sea, from distant *galaxies,* and from *prehistoric* times.

Recently, Spielberg focused on a different *category* of monster. He paid *homage* to his Jewish background with the *creation* of *Schindler's List*, a moving and terrifying story about the Holocaust. People used to say that Spielberg would never grow up, that his movies would always help us hold onto our childhood fantasies. As *Schindler's List* indicates, no one stays a child forever.

UNDERSTANDING THE STORY

>>>> *Circle the letter next to each correct statement.*

1. The statement that best expresses the main idea of this selection is:
   a. Steven Spielberg has always liked to make movies.
   b. Spielberg's movies focus on his lonely childhood.
   c. Spielberg is fascinated by technology.

2. From this story, you can conclude that
   a. Steven Spielberg feels most comfortable behind a camera.
   b. Spielberg uses technology to convert other people's ideas into movie characters.
   c. Spielberg will probably not make any more fantasy movies.

MAKE AN ALPHABETICAL LIST

>>>> *Here are the ten vocabulary words in this lesson. Write them in alphabetical order in the spaces below.*

repulsive	antagonize	caliber	prehistoric	homage
galaxies	creation	category	evolved	endearing

1. _____   6. _____

2. _____   7. _____

3. _____   8. _____

4. _____   9. _____

5. _____   10. _____

WHAT DO THE WORDS MEAN?

>>>> *Following are some meanings, or definitions, for the ten vocabulary words in this lesson. Write the words next to their definitions.*

1. _____ before written history began

2. _____ charming; causing an emotional attachment

3. _____ tribute; respect

4. _____ clusters of stars that make up the universe

5. _____ developed; changed

6. _____ disgusting

7. _____ to bother, upset, or oppose

8. _____ level of excellence; quality

9. _____ the act of bringing something into existence

10. _____ a division or classification

FIND THE ANALOGIES

>>>> In an **analogy,** the relationship between one pair of words is the same as the relationship between another pair of words. For example, here is one kind of analogy: *dog* is to *friendly* as *feeling* is to *uncomfortable.* In this relationship, the first word in each pair is an object or idea, and the second word in each pair describes the object or idea.

>>>> *See if you can complete the following analogies. Circle the correct word.*

1. **Monster** is to **repulsive** as **caliber** is to

   a. disgusting   b. high   c. alien   d. rifle

2. **Movie** is to **engaging** as **animal** is to

   a. prehistoric   b. plant   c. cinema   d. category

3. **Species** are to **evolved** as **galaxies** are to

   a. antagonized   b. changed   c. unexplored   d. endangered

4. **Category** is to **separate** as **creation** is to

   a. new   b. classified   c. development   d. homage

USE YOUR OWN WORDS

>>>> *Look at the picture. What words come into your mind other than the ten vocabulary words used in this lesson? Write them on the lines below. To help you get started, here are two good words:*

1. ____director____
2. ____ashes____
3. _____
4. _____
5. _____
6. _____
7. _____
8. _____
9. _____
10. _____

MAKE POSSESSIVE WORDS

>>>> The singular possessive of a word shows that something belongs to it. For example, Bill has a boat, so it is *Bill's* boat. To make a possessive of a word that is singular, add an apostrophe and an *s* to the word, such as *baker's* bread or *class's* teacher. To make a possessive of a plural word that ends in *s*, add an apostrophe only, such as *friends'* bicycles or *ladies'* hats. To make a possessive of a plural word that does not end in *s*, add an apostrophe and an *s*, such as *children's* toys.

>>>> *Here are ten words from the story. In the space next to the word, write its correct possessive form.*

1. creation _____
2. Spielberg _____
3. family _____
4. sisters _____
5. bullies _____

6. galaxies _____
7. movies _____
8. theater _____
9. series _____
10. Anne _____

COMPLETE THE STORY

>>>> Here are the ten vocabulary words for this lesson:

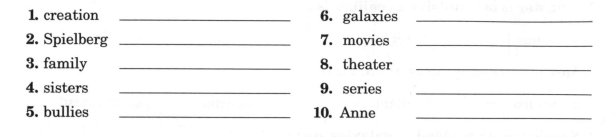

| homage | caliber | antagonize | repulsive | galaxies |
| prehistoric | category | creation | evolved | endearing |

>>>> *There are seven blanks in the story below. Three vocabulary words have already been used in the story. They are underlined. Use the other seven words to fill in the blanks.*

Steven Spielberg's movies do not fall into just one _____. Some of his creatures traveled to us from distant _____ and some lived long ago in _____ times. Some of his characters are ugly and _____, while others are <u>endearing</u>. Spielberg has received many awards that pay <u>homage</u> to the high _____ of his work. His <u>creation</u> of *The Color Purple* and *Schindler's List* has helped us examine our past and the ways in which we _____ each other. As Spielberg's ideas about our world and our relationships have changed and_____, so have his movies.

Learn More About Steven Spielberg

>>>> *On a separate piece of paper or in your notebook or journal, complete one or more of the activities below.*

Learning Across the Curriculum

Think of something you would like to teach others, in the same way that Spielberg used *Schindler's List* to help people learn about the Holocaust. Outline a movie script on the topic.

Broadening Your Understanding

Spielberg created different types of action films using the latest technology. Research the use of special effects in movies today. Share your information with the class.

Extending Your Reading

Read one of the following Spielberg biographies:

Steven Spielberg, Amazing Filmmaker, by Jim Hargrove
The Picture Life of Steven Spielberg, by Michael Leather

Describe events and people in Spielberg's early life that helped shape his movies, such as his father's work as an electrical engineer.

17 ROLLER COASTER MANIA

It blasts off with a roar, and within four heart-stopping seconds, riders are *hurtled* along steel tracks at 70 miles per hour. Zooming vertically 141 feet up, they speed over and under loops, through corkscrew curves, and around hairpin turns. Screams and screeches *punctuate* the air. Rollercoaster *mania* is sweeping the land. No one wants to *stifle* it.

In the last few years, there's been a *surge* of interest in roller coasters. Amusement parks are jumping. Roller coasters are the *lure.*

All roller coasters work on the same principle. An electric motor drives a *conveyor* chain that moves a train of cars up the first loop. After that, gravity pulls them down steep hills and around curves.

The first roller coaster was invented in 1866 by LaMarcus Thompson. Because of his *insomnia,* he spent many nights working on his idea. Roller coasters began to spring up all over the United States. The Cyclone at Coney Island was the wildest. The famous Loop-the-Loop was a thriller. The person who designed it alerted newspapers to send photographers to catch the proof on film. A glass of water he had placed in one of the cars did not spill as it went through a loop!

Today, there are three great roller coasters. One is the Loch Ness Monster, with *vertical* *aerial* loops. The other is the Mind Bender, with a spectacular triple loop. The Corkscrew is the other favorite. It appears to throw riders into the lake below. The thrill of the roller coaster seems to be one that many people enjoy.

UNDERSTANDING THE STORY

>>>> *Circle the letter next to each correct statement.*

1. The statement that best expresses the main idea of this selection is:
   a. Roller coasters are dangerous.
   b. Roller coasters are strongly and safely constructed.
   c. A new interest in roller coasters has developed over the past several years.

2. From this story, you can conclude that
   a. more amusement parks will want roller coasters because they draw big crowds.
   b. newer roller coasters will be made of plastic and fiberglass.
   c. some amusement parks will never have roller coasters.

MAKE AN ALPHABETICAL LIST

>>>> *Here are the ten vocabulary words in this lesson. Write them in alphabetical order in the spaces below.*

hurtled	stifle	punctuate	conveyor	surge
aerial	lure	vertical	insomia	mania

1. _____
2. _____
3. _____
4. _____
5. _____

6. _____
7. _____
8. _____
9. _____
10. _____

WHAT DO THE WORDS MEAN?

>>>> *Following are some meanings, or definitions, for the ten vocabulary words in this lesson. Write the words next to their definitions.*

1. _____ sleeplessness; inability to sleep

2. _____ endless moving belt; carrier

3. _____ moved with great force; sped

4. _____ craze; tremendous excitement

5. _____ to mark or divide; to interrupt

6. _____ upright; straight up and down

7. _____ sudden strong rush; quick buildup

8. _____ attraction; temptation

9. _____ to stop; hold back

10. _____ relating to the air

FIND THE ANALOGIES

>>>> In an **analogy,** similar relationships occur between words that are different. For example, *pig* is to *hog* as *car* is to *automobile*. The relationship is that the words mean the same. Here's another analogy: *noisy* is to *quiet* as *short* is to *tall*. In this relationship, the words have opposite meanings.

>>>> *See if you can complete the following analogies. Circle the correct word.*

1. **Vertical** is to **horizontal** as **sleepy** is to

    a. wakeful   b. practical   c. hazy   d. tense

2. **Stifle** is to **stop** as **labor** is to

    a. rest   b. fight   c. work   d. decide

3. **Punctuate** is to **interrupt** as **hurtle** is to

    a. throw   b. speed   c. creep   d. decline

4. **Surge** is to **rise** as **lure** is to

    a. attract   b. live   c. fly   d. lunge

5. **Mania** is to **craze** as **depression** is to

    a. interest   b. sadness   c. happiness   d. holiness

USE YOUR OWN WORDS

>>>> *Look at the picture. What words come into your mind other than the ten vocabulary words used in this lesson? Write them on the lines below. To help you get started, here are two good words:*

1. thrilling

2. terrifying

3. _____

4. _____

5. _____

6. _____

7. _____

8. _____

9. _____

10. _____

FIND THE SUBJECTS AND PREDICATES

>>>> The **subject** of a sentence names the person, place, or thing that is spoken about. The **predicate** of a sentence is what is said about the subject. For example:

> The small boy went to the football game.

>>>> *The small boy* is the subject (the person the sentence is about), and *went to the football game* is the predicate of the sentence (because it tells what the small boy did).

>>>> *In the following sentences, draw one line under the subject of the sentence and two lines under the predicate of the sentence.*

1. The new roller coasters zoom into hairpin turns and aerial loops.
2. It takes a week to complete all of the games and rides in an amusement park.
3. Curving into corkscrew turns, the new roller coaster frightened its passengers.
4. Inventors are busy at their drawing boards creating faster, larger roller coasters.
5. Climbing upright to 140 feet, the roller coaster slowed down.

COMPLETE THE STORY

>>>> Here are the ten vocabulary words for this lesson:

punctuated	hurtled	vertically	surge	stifle
conveyor	insomnia	aerial	lure	mania

>>>> *There are seven blank spaces in the story below. Three vocabulary words have already been used in the story. They are underlined. Use the other seven words to fill in the blanks.*

The roller coaster <u>hurtled</u> along on its endless belt. At 100 miles per hour, it zoomed in a _____ climb. The riders were frightened. Their screams _____ the air. The _____ chain belt stopped suddenly. The worried passengers tried to _____ their fears until the roller coaster started again.

This description explains how amusement parks <u>lure</u> their customers to their exciting rides. There has been a recent _____ of interest in roller coasters. The public loves the _____ loops that the roller coasters perform. There is a <u>mania</u> for this wild ride all over the United States. The inventor of the roller coaster suffered from _____. It was during his wakeful nights that he created the amusement park's hottest attraction.

Learn More About Park Rides

>>>> *On a separate piece of paper or in your notebook or journal, complete one or more of the activities below.*

Learning Across the Curriculum

Discover how roller coasters work. How can a roller coaster do a loop and keep everyone safe? After you find out more about the science behind roller coasters, design your own ride. Make sure riders will stay safe while they're on your ride.

Broadening Your Understanding

Why do people like roller coasters so much? Interview five of your friends who have ridden on a roller coaster. Then write why they like or dislike it. Also find out reasons why roller coasters appeal to so many people.

Extending Your Reading

Find out more about amusement parks by reading one of the following books. Then write what makes amusement parks so popular.

Window on Main Street, by Tim O'Brien
The American Amusement Park Industry, by Judith Adams
Amusement Parks: An American Guidebook, by John Norris
Step Right Up, Folks!, by Al Griffin

Louise Nevelson was one of the greatest modern **sculptors.** Geometric art of **colossal** proportions was the foundation of her work. Her sculptures **adorn** parks, squares, and buildings all over America. Her pieces have been shown at New York's Whitney Museum and Museum of Modern Art, as well as at numerous other well-known galleries. She assembled found objects from junk piles for her sculptures. Wooden boxes, spiral pieces, and triangles are some of the things she used, arranging the objects in **collages.** She often built them to seemingly **excessive** heights.

Nevelson was born in Russia. Her family emigrated to the United States to escape **hostile** attitudes against Jews. At an early age, she knew she wanted to be an artist. When she finished her schooling, she moved to New York to study art. As a sculptor, Nevelson worked hard at her craft, but didn't gain success until she was 60 years old, when museums began to buy her work. This success was a **milestone** in her career. Nevelson felt she had lived up to her artistic **potential.** Although her success came late in life, she had a long career. She died in 1988 at the age of 88.

Nevelson was totally committed to her work of creating great art from odds and ends. She was considered the mother of **environmental** sculpture. During her **distinguished** career, she used her considerable talent to enrich this world and create a new world from her imagination.

UNDERSTANDING THE STORY

>>>> *Circle the letter next to each correct statement.*

1. The statement that best expresses the main idea of this selection is:
   a. Louise Nevelson was a sculptor who was easily influenced by the works of others.
   b. Louise Nevelson's parents helped her become a sculptor by encouraging her.
   c. Louise Nevelson attained fame and success because she didn't allow anything to stand in the way of her talent.

2. From this story, you can conclude that
   a. emigrant artists will continue to become famous in America.
   b. Louise Nevelson's fame and influence in the art world will continue to grow.
   c. Louise Nevelson will continue exploring new realms of artistic expression.

MAKE AN ALPHABETICAL LIST

>>>> *Here are the ten vocabulary words in this lesson. Write them in alphabetical order in the spaces below.*

adorn	collages	hostile	excessive	potential
milestone	colossal	distinguished	environmental	sculptors

1. _____
2. _____
3. _____
4. _____
5. _____

6. _____
7. _____
8. _____
9. _____
10. _____

WHAT DO THE WORDS MEAN?

>>>> *Following are some meanings, or definitions, for the ten vocabulary words in this lesson. Write the words next to their definitions.*

1. _____ decorate; ornament

2. _____ artists; carvers

3. _____ too much

4. _____ huge; gigantic

5. _____ art works of different materials pasted on a surface

6. _____ unfriendly; angry

7. _____ noted; marked by excellence

8. _____ an important point in development; worthy achievement

9. _____ describing surroundings; total background or atmosphere

10. _____ the ability to do or become

FIND THE ANALOGIES

>>>> In an **analogy,** similar relationships occur between words that are different. For example, *pig* is to *hog* as *car* is to *automobile*. The relationship is that the words mean the same. Here's another analogy: *noisy* is to *quiet* as *short* is to *tall*. In this relationship, the words have opposite meanings.

>>>> *See if you can complete the following analogies. Circle the correct word.*

1. Adorn is to **beautify** as **destroy** is to

    a. love   b. exterminate   c. decorate   d. illustrate

2. Potential is to **uselessness** as **adore** is to

    a. love   b. despise   c. settle   d. confuse

3. Colossal is to **enormous** as **minute** is to

    a. second   b. huge   c. tiny   d. medium

4. Hostility is to **friendship** as **contempt** is to

    a. affection   b. illusion   c. difference   d. selfishness

5. Distinguished is to **unimportant** as **wise** is to

    a. intelligent   b. stupid   c. fortunate   d. greedy

USE YOUR OWN WORDS

>>>> *Look at the picture. What words come into your mind other than the ten vocabulary words used in this lesson? Write them on the lines below. To help you get started, here are two good words:*

1. _____ expressive _____
2. _____ abstract _____
3. _____
4. _____
5. _____
6. _____
7. _____
8. _____
9. _____
10. _____

FIND THE SUBJECTS AND PREDICATES

>>>> The **subject** of a sentence names the person, place, or thing that is spoken about. The **predicate** of a sentence is what is said about the subject. For example:

The small boy went to the football game.

The small boy is the subject (the person the sentence is about), and *went to the football game* is the predicate of the sentence (because it tells what the small boy did).

>>>> *In the following sentences, draw one line under the subject of the sentence and two lines under the predicate of the sentence.*

1. Some artists like to arrange their works in the form of collages.
2. The Whitney Museum had a display of Nevelson's work.
3. An artist can work in stone, wood, paint, pencil, ink, or paper.
4. Talent is a rare gift that few people have.
5. Artists express what they feel about the world through their works.

COMPLETE THE STORY

>>>> Here are the ten vocabulary words for this lesson:

potential	environmental	milestone	distinguished	excessive
sculptors	colossal	adorn	hostile	collages

>>>> *There are seven blank spaces in the story below. Three vocabulary words have already been used in the story. They are underlined. Use the other seven words to fill in the blanks.*

Louise Nevelson reached a _____ in her career. She might never have realized her artistic _____ if her family had not emigrated from Russia, where they had often faced _____ neighbors.

After studying all the arts, the work of _____ appealed to Nevelson most. Her art involved arranging different objects and materials in collages. Some critics have said that she constructed her figures to excessive heights.

Her sculptures are _____ in size. They are also environmental because they create a world of their own. Nevelson's monumental works _____ parks, museums, and public squares in many cities. She is thought of as one of the most _____ sculptors in the world.

Learn More About Sculpture

>>>> *On a separate piece of paper or in your notebook or journal, complete one or more of the activities below.*

Appreciating Diversity

Find a sculptor who shares your heritage. Look at some of his or her work and find out what you can about him or her. Then write how you think the sculptor's background influenced—or did not influence—his or her work.

Learning Across the Curriculum

One of Louise Nevelson's techniques was to use objects she found to create sculpture. Go on a walk and collect some objects. Create a sculpture with them and display your sculpture in the classroom.

Broadening Your Understanding

Go to a museum or gallery in your town. Look at some sculpture. (If you cannot locate any sculpture in your area, find picures in books.) Find a sculptor whose work you like and find out more about him or her. Write about his or her history and the style or medium in which he or she works and what the sculptor is trying to show with his or her work.

The press called him "Captain Outrageous." He earned that nickname during the America's Cup yacht races. Ted Turner had a reputation for being a fearless and resourceful sailor. He defended the America's Cup and received worldwide praise. But he gained more notice for his behavior. He had no patience for mistakes or routine efforts. He would taunt his crew and question their skill. His crew, however, seemed to respond to his inspiration and daring. Turner's methods worked. In 1977 his yacht, Courageous, successfully defended the America's Cup, winning yacht racing's top prize.

That was the first time that many people heard of Ted Turner. He now owns the MGM library of 3,650 films, including Gone With the Wind and The Wizard of Oz. Turner has made the controversial decision to colorize some of the black-and-white films. He believes that color will make the films more popular and give them a wider audience. Many people disapprove of such tactics, but Turner continues to use the process. The turbulent debate over colorization will undoubtedly continue for a long time.

Today, Ted Turner's fame and future are tied up with cable television. His Cable News Network (CNN) has caused a revolution in TV. His 24-hour-a-day news service is said to be viewed in the majority of homes in the United States. Few people thought that a 24-hour news service could embrace so wide an audience. Turner is also the proprietor of two other popular cable stations—Turner Network Television (TNT) and Turner Broadcasting System (TBS). Ted Turner has proven himself to be a winner.

UNDERSTANDING THE STORY

>>>> *Circle the letter next to each correct statement.*

1. The statement that best expresses the main idea of this selection is:
   a. Ted Turner has the ability to be outstanding in many fields.
   b. If you are talented in one field, you can be talented in others.
   c. Cable News Network has caused a minor revolution in TV.

2. From this story, you can conclude that
   a. Ted Turner is satisfied with the activities he has done.
   b. Ted Turner will return to yacht racing.
   c. Ted Turner feels that there are always new fields to conquer.

MAKE AN ALPHABETICAL LIST

>>>> *Here are the ten vocabulary words in this lesson. Write them in alphabetical order in the spaces below.*

embrace	outrageous	fearless	tactics	resourceful
turbulent	routine	proprietor	taunt	inspiration

1. _____
2. _____
3. _____
4. _____
5. _____

6. _____
7. _____
8. _____
9. _____
10. _____

WHAT DO THE WORDS MEAN?

>>>> *Following are some meanings, or definitions, for the ten vocabulary words in this lesson. Write the words next to their definitions.*

1. _____ without fear; brave

2. _____ to cover an area or group

3. _____ customary or usual

4. _____ actions taken to gain success

5. _____ wild; disorderly

6. _____ to insult; to mock

7. _____ unusually shocking

8. _____ an action or thought that moves one to greater efforts

9. _____ able to deal skillfully with new situations

10. _____ owner of a business

FIND THE ANALOGIES

>>>> In an **analogy**, similar relationships occur between words that are different. For example, *pig* is to *hog* as *car* is to *automobile*. The relationship is that the words mean the same. Here's another analogy: *noisy* is to *quiet* as *short* is to *tall*. In this relationship, the words have opposite meanings.

>>>> *See if you can complete the following analogies. Circle the correct word.*

1. **Fearless** is to **cowardly** as **turbulent** is to

   a. distressed   b. foolish   c. violent   d. calm

2. **Proprietor** is to **employee** as **landlord** is to

   a. owner   b. supervisor   c. tenant   d. government

3. **Resourceful** is to **quick thinking** as **routine** is to

   a. unknown   b. shocking   c. unusual   d. ordinary

4. **Embrace** is to **reject** as **attract** is to

   a. repel   b. lure   c. comfort   d. engage

5. **Outrageous** is to **shocking** as **laborious** is to

   a. cheerful   b. incorrect   c. delightful   d. difficult

USE YOUR OWN WORDS

>>>> *Look at the picture. What words come into your mind other than the ten vocabulary words used in this lesson? Write them on the lines below. To help you get started, here are two good words:*

1. _____ confident _____
2. _____ crew _____
3. _____
4. _____
5. _____
6. _____
7. _____
8. _____
9. _____
10. _____

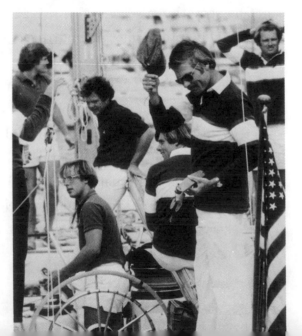

DESCRIBE THE NOUNS

>>>> *Two of the vocabulary words, tactics and proprietor, are nouns. List as many words as you can that describe or tell something about the words tactics and proprietor. You can work on this with your classmates. Listed below are some words to help you get started.*

tactics

1. _____ military _____
2. _____ clever _____
3. _____
4. _____
5. _____
6. _____

proprietor

1. _____ responsible _____
2. _____ creative _____
3. _____
4. _____
5. _____
6. _____

COMPLETE THE STORY

>>>> Here are the ten vocabulary words for this lesson:

turbulent	routine	taunt	outrageous	proprietor
tactics	inspiration	resourceful	embrace	fearless

>>>> *There are seven blank spaces in the story below. Three vocabulary words have already been used in the story. They are underlined. Use the other seven words to fill in the blanks.*

One can never tell what Ted Turner will do next. Whatever he does, it surely will not be something _____. On the basis of his past performance, it is more likely to be something <u>outrageous</u>. Turner's techniques in business and in sports have gained him worldwide attention. As a yachtsman, he has shown himself to be a _____ sailor who served as an <u>inspiration</u> to his crew. Some people did not approve of Turner's behavior because he would _____ his crew in public. However, his unusual _____ produced the desired results. His yacht won the America's Cup.

Turner has been just as <u>resourceful</u> in the _____ world of television. As _____ of the Cable News Network, he took a gamble with a 24-hour-a-day news service. Few people thought that this idea would _____ such a large audience. The critics were wrong.

114

Learn More About Ted Turner

>>>> *On a separate piece of paper or in your notebook or journal, complete one or more of the activities below.*

Building Language

Watch a newscast in your native language. Now, watch one in English. Explain the differences between the newscasts. What are the reasons for the differences? If you cannot find a newscast in your native language, compare a newspaper written in your native language to one written in English.

Learning Across the Curriculum

Colorization is a fairly new process. Research how it is done. Write a report that describes how colorization works and that explains its history. If you can, rent the colorized and uncolorized versions of a film, such as *The Philadelphia Story*. Which version did you like better?

Broadening Your Understanding

Ted Turner has used his position as head of a network to create shows that follow his interests. For example, he created a cartoon series about environmentalism and several dramatic series about Native Americans. Imagine that you have your own network. What issue would you most like people to know about? How would you present the information in a series that would interest people and make them think about the topic? Write a memo to a TV executive, proposing your ideas.

20 ZANZIBAR

Zanzibar was once a land of pirates and slave traders. A $\boxed{\textit{bazaar}}$ marked the center of activity. Ivory, turquoise, and silver were sold and so were human beings. Zanzibar was a busy, $\boxed{\textit{exotic}}$ town filled with drama. In the 19th century, it was known as the $\boxed{\textit{metropolis}}$ of East Africa. People came to visit from all over the world.

Both the town of Zanzibar and the island on which it is $\boxed{\textit{situated}}$ have the same name. It is off the east coast of Africa in the Indian Ocean. This location is the important key to its history.

The Portuguese arrived in Zanzibar in the late 15th century. They were looking for a trade route to the Indies. A hundred years later, the Portuguese made Zanzibar a trading $\boxed{\textit{depot}}$ for $\boxed{\textit{commerce}}$ with Africa. Zanzibar later came under Arab, then British, control.

The world has changed since those colorful days. The slave trade was $\boxed{\textit{suppressed}}$ more than 100 years ago. Zanzibar is no longer under the influence of foreign rulers. It is part of the United Republic of Tanzania, a country formed by $\boxed{\textit{uniting}}$ Tanganyika, on the African continent, with the island state of Zanzibar. Today's traveler finds Zanzibar a shabby town with none of the glamour it knew in the past.

Although nobody would want Zanzibar to return to the time when it was filled with pirates and slave traders, many people do long for a more exciting Zanzibar. Plans are underway to restore old buildings and to bring back some of the atmosphere of the old bazaar. People in Zanzibar hope to develop the town's economy and $\boxed{\textit{entice}}$ $\boxed{\textit{tourists}}$ to visit.

UNDERSTANDING THE STORY

>>>> *Circle the letter next to each correct statement.*

1. The statement that best expresses the main idea of this selection is:
   a. Zanzibar is situated on an island in the Indian Ocean off the coast of Africa.
   b. Today, Zanzibar is part of Tanzania and is very much the same as it has always been.
   c. Zanzibar's present is very different from its past, and some people want to bring back just a bit of the past.

2. From this story, you can conclude that
   a. people are sorry that Zanzibar is no longer ruled by foreigners.
   b. Zanzibar has been influenced by Europeans, Arabs, and Africans.
   c. a lot of tourists have visited Zanzibar in the last 20 years.

117

MAKE AN ALPHABETICAL LIST

>>>> *Here are the ten vocabulary words in this lesson. Write them in alphabetical order in the spaces below.*

tourists	situated	exotic	depot	bazaar
commerce	uniting	suppressed	metropolis	entice

1. _____

2. _____

3. _____

4. _____

5. _____

6. _____

7. _____

8. _____

9. _____

10. _____

WHAT DO THE WORDS MEAN?

>>>> *Following are some meanings, or definitions, for the ten vocabulary words in this lesson. Write the words next to their definitions.*

1. _____ put an end to; to keep down or under tight control

2. _____ located

3. _____ large city; important center of culture or trade

4. _____ people who travel for pleasure

5. _____ marketplace with streets lined with stalls or shops

6. _____ collecting station; warehouse or storehouse

7. _____ joining together

8. _____ business; trade

9. _____ to attract; to tempt

10. _____ of another part of the world; foreign; strange

FIND THE ANALOGIES

>>>> In an **analogy,** similar relationships occur between words that are different. For example, *pig* is to *hog* as *car* is to *automobile.* The relationship is that the words mean the same. Here's another analogy: *noisy* is to *quiet* as *short* is to *tall.* In this relationship, the words have opposite meanings.

>>>> *See if you can complete the following analogies. Circle the correct word.*

1. **Bazaar** is to **marketplace** as **attorney** is to

    a. scientist   b. lawyer   c. officer   d. accountant

2. **Uniting** is to **separating** as **admitting** is to

    a. confessing   b. saying   c. denying   d. wondering

3. **Commerce** is to **trade** as **tourist** is to

    a. inhabitant   b. traveler   c. airplane   d. announcer

4. **Metropolis** is to **city** as **robot** is to

    a. machine   b. science   c. living   d. symptom

5. **Exotic** is to **ordinary** as **courageous** is to

    a. heroic   b. ancient   c. deadly   d. fearful

USE YOUR OWN WORDS

>>>> *Look at the picture. What words come into your mind other than the ten vocabulary words used in this lesson? Write them on the lines below. To help you get started, here are two good words:*

1. _____ obsolete _____

2. _____ vivid _____

3. _____

4. _____

5. _____

6. _____

7. _____

8. _____

9. _____

10. _____

IDENTIFY THE SYNONYMS AND ANTONYMS

>>>> *There are six vocabular words listed below. To the right of each is either a synonym or an antonym. Remember: a synonym is a word that means the same or nearly the same as another word. An antonym is a word that means the opposite of another word. On the line beside each pair of words, write S for synonyms and A for antonyms.*

1.	**commerce**	business	1.	_____
2.	**tourists**	residents	2.	_____
3.	**depot**	storchouse	3.	_____
4.	**entice**	attract	4.	_____
5.	**suppressed**	started	5.	_____
6.	**situated**	located	6.	_____

COMPLETE THE STORY

>>>> Here are the ten vocabulary words for this lesson:

depot	tourists	bazaar	commerce	situated
exotic	suppressed	metropolis	uniting	entice

>>>> *There are seven blank spaces in the story below. Three vocabulary words have already been used in the story. They are underlined. Use the other seven words to fill in the blanks.*

Zanzibar is _____ on an island off the coast of East Africa. When the Europeans came to Zanzibar hundreds of years ago, they made Zanzibar a trading _____ for underline:commerce with the African continent.

Modern Zanzibar is part of the Republic of Tanzania. It was formed by _____ Tanganyika on the mainland and the island state of Zanzibar. Today, Zanzibar is no longer the booming _____ it once was. The slave trade was _____ decades ago. The busy _____ no longer lines the streets. There has been little to <u>entice</u> many people to visit Zanzibar. The <u>exotic</u> atmosphere of the town has gone with the changes that have taken place. Perhaps the restoration of the old town will make Zanzibar a more exciting place for _____ to visit.

Learn More About Zanzibar

>>>> *On a separate piece of paper or in your notebook or journal, complete one or more of the activities below.*

Learning Across the Curriculum

Research the history of Zanzibar. Take note of the major events in the town's history. Write a timeline that includes each key event. If you can, enhance your timeline with illustrations or photographs.

Broadening Your Understanding

You have just been put in charge of Zanzibar's new campaign to attract tourists. Research what Zanzibar is like now and some of its history. Write a brochure that makes the most of Zanzibar's past and shows visitors the town's current attractions.

Extending Your Reading

Read more about what recent travelers have found in Zanzibar. Then write why you would or would not include Zanzibar on a list of places you'd like to visit.

Man Eaters Motel and Other Stops on the Railway to Nowhere, by Denis Boyles
Zanzibar to Timbuktu, by Anthony Daniels

Glossary

A

accuracy *[AK yuh ruh see]* correctness; skillfulness

acknowledged *[ak NAHL ijd]* generally recognized or accepted

adorn *[uh DORN]* decorate, ornament

adversity *[ad VUR sih tee]* misfortune; bad luck; hardship

advocated *[AD voh kay tid]* favored; recommended

aerial *[AIR ee ul]* relating to the air

afflictions *[uh FLIK shuhnz]* pain or suffering

analysis *[uh NAL uh sihs]* breaking something complex into parts and examining the parts

antagonize *[an TAG uh neyez]* to bother, upset, or oppose

arrogant *[AIR uh gunt]* proud; acting superior

articulate *[ar TIK yoo liht]* skilled in using language

assets *[AS ehts]* resources; advantages

astonishing *[uh STON ish ing]* amazing; surprising

audible *[AW duh buhl]* capable of being heard

audition *[aw DIHSH uhn]* to try out for something

avail *[uh VAYL]* of use or advantage

avert *[uh VEHRT]* to prevent something from happening; to avoid

B

bazaar *[buh ZAR]* marketplace with streets lined with stalls or shops

bindings *[BYND ings]* covers and backings for holding book pages together

bombards *[bom BARDZ]* attacks strongly

C

caliber *[KAL uh buhr]* level of excellence; quality

capitalize *[KAP uh tuhl eyez]* to make the most of something

captions *[KAP shuhns]* printed explanations of pictures; dialogue printed on the screen during a movie or television show

captivate *[KAP tuh vayt]* to charm; to capture someone's interest

catastrophe *[kuh TAS truh fee]* disaster; tragedy

category *[KAT uh gohr ee]* a division or classification

cavorted *[kuh VORT id]* ran and jumped around playfully

celebrated *[SEL uh brayt id]* famous; renowned

celebrity *[suh LEB ruh tee]* a famous person

chided *[CHEYE duhd]* spoke out in anger or disapproval

cinema *[SIHN uh muh]* motion-picture theater

collaborated *[kuh LAB ur rayt id]* worked together; cooperated

collages *[kuh LAJ iz]* art works of different materials pasted on a surface

colossal *[kuh LAH sohl]* huge, gigantic

commerce *[KAHM urs]* business; trade

commodity *[kuh MAWD uh tee]* a product; something useful

computed *[kuhm PYOOT uhd]* figured out; calculated

confined *[kon FYND]* restricted to a particular place

considers *[kon SIHD urs]* believes; thinks of; regards

conspicuous *[kon SPIK yoo us]* easily seen; attracting attention

constructed *[kon STRUKT id]* built; made

contemplated *[KON tuhm playt uhd]* considered; thought about

continuity *[KON tih nyoo ih tee]* an unbroken flow; progression

convert *[KON vurt]* a new believer; a new follower

conveyor *[kon VAY ir]* endless moving belt; carrier

coordination *[koh OR duh nay shun]* the act of helping a complex process work smoothly

creation *[kree AY shuhn]* the act of bringing something into existence

creativity *[kree ay TIV ih tee]* imagination; originality; artistic talent

D

data *[DAYT uh]* information

dejected *[de JEKT ehd]* depressed

delirious *[dih LIR ee us]* wildly excited; enthusiastic, emotional

demon *[DEE mun]* an evil spirit; devil

dependent *[dih PEN dent]* to be reliant on other people or things for what is needed

depot *[DEE poh]* collecting station; warehouse or storehouse

descent *[dih SENT]* ancestry; origin

desolate *[DEH soh let]* lonely; abandoned, miserable

destitute *[DEH stih toot]* poor, needy; deprived

determined *[dih TUR munhd]* having one's mind made up; strong willed

disability *[dis uh BIL uh tee]* a disadvantage that makes activities very difficult

disbelief *[DIS buh leef]* rejection of something as untrue

disconnected *[dis kuhn NEKT uhd]* separated

discrimination *[dis KRIM ih nay shun]* prejudice; acting unfairly against someone

disrupted *[dis RUPT uhd]* threw into disorder

distinguished *[dis TING wishd]* noted; marked by excellence

divorced *[dih VORSD]* no longer married

dominant *[DOM uh nint]* commanding

dominate *[DOM uh NAYT]* control; rule

dramatic *[druh MAT ik]* theatrical; describing acting ability

dynamic *[dy NAM ik]* forceful; energetic; active

E

eclipsed *[eh KLIPSED]* went beyond; overshadowed

elementary [el uh MEN tur ee] fundamental or simplest part

embrace [em BRAYS] to cover an area or group

emigrants [EM ih grants] people who leave one country to settle in another

emphasized [EM fah syzd] stressed; made important

encouragement [en KUR ij munt] support

endearing [en DIR ing] charming; causing an emotional attachment

enrolled [en ROHLD] entered; joined; registered

enterprise [EN tur PRYZ] a difficult or complicated project

entice [en TYS] to attract; to tempt

envelops [en VEH lops] surrounds; wraps around

environmental [en vy run MEN tul] describing surroundings; total background or atmosphere

evolved [ee VOLVD] developed; changed

exception [eks SEP shon] different; one of a kind

excessive [eks SES iv] too much

exclusive [eks KLOO siv] one and only; open only to the upper classes or the wealthy

existence [eks IS tense] life; being

exotic [eg ZOT ik] of another part of the world; foreign; strange

expectations [ek spek TAY shuns] hopes, prospects

F

facial [FAY shul] of or relating to the face

facilities [fuh SIL uh tees] equipment to help people do things more easily

fantastic [fan TAS tik] unbelievable; amazing

fearless [FEAR les] without fear; brave

flair [FLAIR] a skill or talent

focus [FOH kus] the center of attention

forbidding [for BIH ding] frightening; fearful

G

galaxies [GAL uhk sees] clusters of stars that make up the universe

groomed [GROOMD] combed and brushed; rubbed down

H

harsh [HARSH] severe; sometimes even hostile

homage [AWM ihj] tribute; respect

hostile [HOS til] unfriendly; angry

hurtled [HUR tuld] moved with great force; sped

I

illustrated [IL uh STRAYT id] created pictures or drawings

inadequate [in AD ih kwit] not good enough; lacking; below par

incapacitated [in cuh PAH si ta tud] unable to function in some way

incurable [in KYOOR uh bul] not able to be healed or cured

indebted [ihn DET ihd] owing something to someone

indelible [ihn DEL uh buhl] something that cannot be removed or erased

indispensable [ihn dih SPEHN suh buhl] essential; absolutely necessary

infantry [IHN fuhn tree] soldiers who fight on foot

innovative [IN uh VAY tiv] able to do things in a new way; creative

insomnia [in SOM nee ah] sleeplessness; inability to sleep

inspiration [in spir AY shun] an action or thought that moves one to greater efforts

instantaneously [ihn stuhn TAY nee uhs lee] without any delay

irresistible [ihr rih ZIS tuh buhl] having a strong appeal or attraction

J

jubilant [JOO bih lint] filled with great joy; extremely happy

L

legitimate [luh JIHT uh muht] not false; legal; justified

limitless [LIM it les] never ending; without limit

lobby [LOB ee] a pressure group; a special-interest group to influence lawmakers

luminous [LOO muh nuhs] glowing

lure [LOOR] attraction; temptation

M

malicious [muh LIHSH uhs] seeking to cause harm

mania [MAY nee ah] craze; tremendous excitement

mechanism [MEK uh nihz um] a process or technique that achieves a certain result

melancholy [MEH lun kah lee] sad; gloomy

mellifluous [muh LIF loo wus] musical; flowing

metropolis [meh TRO pul is] large city; important center of culture or trade

milestone [MEYEL stohn] an important point in development; worthy achievement

mistrust [mihs TRUST] a lack of confidence; uncertainty

mute [MYOOT] unable to speak; silent

N

nationality [nash uh NAL uh tee] membership in the cultural group of a particular nation

O

obsolete [ob suh LEET] no longer in use; out of fashion

oppressed [OH presd] persecuted; crushed; overburdened

optimistic [awp tuh MIHS tihk] expecting excellent results

organization [or guh nih ZAY shun] system; structure; plan

outrageous [out RAY jus] unusually shocking

overcome [oh vur CUM] to defeat; to get the better of

overwhelming [oh vur WEHL ming] overpowering

P

participated [par TIH suh pay tid] became actively involved; took part in; cooperated

particles [PAR tih kulz] minute pieces of matter

perceived [puhr SEEVD] understood

perceptible *[puhr SEP tuh bul]* capable of being seen or noticed

perturbed *[pur TURBD]* upset; troubled

physicist *[FIZ uh sist]* an expert in the science that deals with matter and energy

platoons *[pluh TOONZ]* divisions of a military unit

polio *[POH lee oh]* a crippling disease that paralyzes certain muscles

portraying *[por TRAY ing]* playing the role of; representing

potential *[poh TEN shul]* the ability to do or become

prehistoric *[pree hihs TOR ik]* before written history began

prescribed *[prih SKRYBD]* urged; strongly advised; recommended

priority *[preye OR uh tee]* a position of importance, something that comes first

proprietor *[pruh PRY ih tir]* owner of a business

prosperity *[prah SPER ih tee]* well being or wealth, usually financial

punctuate *[PUNK choo ayt]* to mark or divide; to interrupt

pursuit *[pir SOOT]* effort to secure something; search

R

random *[RAN duhm]* having no clear pattern

raved *[RAYVD]* praised highly

regime *[ruh ZHEEM]* the government in power; a form of government

registered *[REJ is turd]* officially enrolled

Republican *[rih PUB lih can]* one of the two major U.S. political parties

repulsive *[ree PULS sihv]* disgusting

requirements *[rih KWIR mints]* things wanted or needed; demands

resided *[rih ZY did]* lived; dwelled

resist *[rih ZIST]* withstand

resourceful *[rih SORS ful]* able to deal skillfully with new situations

routine *[roo TEEN]* customary; usual

S

sculptors *[SKULP tirz]* artists; carvers

similar *[SIM ih lir]* the same; alike

situated *[SICH oo wayt id]* located

soared *[SORD]* moved upward; rose above the ordinary

specialists *[SPESH uhl ihsts]* people who have special training

statistics *[stuh TIS tiks]* field of mathemetics

stifle *[STY ful]* to stop; hold back

suppressed *[suh PRESD]* put an end to; to keep down or under tight control

surge *[SIRJ]* sudden strong rush; quick buildup

surpass *[suhr PAS]* to exceed or go beyond

T

tactics *[TAK tiks]* actions taken to gain success

taunt *[TAWNT]* to insult; to mock

testament *[TES tuh munt]* clear evidence; proof

theoretical *[thee uh RET ih kul]* concerned principally with abstractions and theories

theories *[THIR ez]* ideas about how something might be

thwarted *[THWOHR tuhd]* baffled or opposed effectively

toppled *[TOP uld]* overthrown; pushed over

tourists *[TOOR ists]* people who travel for pleasure

transaction *[tran SAK shun]* communication or business carried out between two parties

transmitting *[trans MIT ing]* sending or transferring from one person or place to another

turbulent *[TIR byoo lint]* wild, disorderly

turmoil *[TUR moil]* confusion

U

unanimously *[yoo NAN ih mus lee]* undisputedly

unattainable *[un ah TAYN uh bul]* out of reach

unification *[yoo nih fih KAY shun]* the bringing together of; consolidation

uniting *[yoo NYT ing]* joining together

upheaval *[up HEE vuhl]* disorder

utilize *[YOO tuh lize]* to use; to employ

V

vacancy *[VAY cun see]* an empty space; an opening

variations *[vair ree AY shunz]* changes; alterations

versions *[VIR zhunz]* points of view; different ways of looking at things

vertical *[VIR tih cul]* upright; straight up and down

views *[VYOOZ]* attitude; opinions

vision *[VIZH un]* something imagined, as in a dream

vivid *[VIV id]* lively; sharp; clear